The Delia Collection
Baking

BBC
BOOKS

Published by BBC Books
BBC Worldwide Ltd
Woodlands
80 Wood Lane
London W12 OTT

First published in 2005

A proportion of these recipes has been published
previously in *Delia Smith The Evening Standard
Cookbook*, *Delia Smith's Book of Cakes*, *Delia
Smith's Complete Illustrated Cookery Course*,
Delia Smith's Winter Collection, *Delia Smith's
Summer Collection*, *Delia's How To Cook Books One,
Two* and *Three*, *Delia Smith's Christmas* and
Delia's Vegetarian Collection.

Edited for BBC Worldwide Ltd
by New Crane Ltd

Editor: Sarah Randell
Designer: Paul Webster
Sub-editor: Heather Cupit
Picture Editor: Diana Hughes
Recipe Testing: Pauline Curran
Commissioning Editor for the BBC: Vivien Bowler

ISBN 0 563 487364

Printed and bound in Italy
by L.E.G.O SpA
Colour separation
by Butler & Tanner

Cover and title page photographs: Peter Knab
For further photographic credits, see page 136

Introduction

When I look back over my years of cookery writing, I have to admit that very often, decisions about what to do have sprung from what my own particular needs are. As a very busy person who has to work, run a home and cook, I felt it was extremely useful to have, for instance, summer recipes in one book – likewise winter and Christmas, giving easy access to those specific seasons.

This, my latest venture, has come about for similar reasons. Thirty five years of recipe writing have produced literally thousands of recipes. So I now feel what would be really helpful is to create a kind of ordered library (so I don't have to rack my brains and wonder which book this or that recipe is in!). Thus, if I want to make a cake, I don't have to look through the baking sections of various books, but have the whole lot in one convenient collection.

In compiling these collections, I have chosen what I think are the best and most popular recipes and, at the same time, have added some that are completely new. It is my hope that those who have not previously tried my recipes will now have smaller collections to sample, and that those dedicated followers will appreciate an ordered library to provide easy access and a reminder of what has gone before and may have been forgotten.

Delia Smith

Conversion Tables

All these are approximate conversions, which have either been rounded up or down. In a few recipes it has been necessary to modify them very slightly. Never mix metric and imperial measures in one recipe, stick to one system or the other.

All spoon measurements used throughout this book are level unless specified otherwise.

All butter is salted unless specified otherwise.

All recipes have been double-tested, using a standard convection oven. If you are using a fan oven, adjust the cooking temperature according to the manufacturer's handbook.

Weights

½ oz	10 g
¾	20
1	25
1½	40
2	50
2½	60
3	75
4	110
4½	125
5	150
6	175
7	200
8	225
9	250
10	275
12	350
1 lb	450
1 lb 8 oz	700
2	900
3	1.35 kg

Volume

2 fl oz	55 ml
3	75
5 (¼ pint)	150
10 (½ pint)	275
1 pint	570
1¼	725
1¾	1 litre
2	1.2
2½	1.5
4	2.25

Dimensions

⅛ inch	3 mm
¼	5
½	1 cm
¾	2
1	2.5
1¼	3
1½	4
1¾	4.5
2	5
2½	6
3	7.5
3½	9
4	10
5	13
5¼	13.5
6	15
6½	16
7	18
7½	19
8	20
9	23
9½	24
10	25.5
11	28
12	30

Oven temperatures

Gas mark 1	275°F	140°C
2	300	150
3	325	170
4	350	180
5	375	190
6	400	200
7	425	220
8	450	230
9	475	240

Contents

Cakes

Preserved Ginger Cake with Lemon Icing

Makes 15 squares

For the cake

5 pieces of preserved stem ginger in syrup, chopped

2 tablespoons ginger syrup (from jar of stem ginger in syrup)

1 heaped teaspoon ground ginger

1 heaped teaspoon grated fresh root ginger

6 oz (175 g) butter, at room temperature, plus a little extra for greasing

6 oz (175 g) golden caster sugar

3 large eggs, at room temperature

1 tablespoon molasses syrup

8 oz (225 g) self-raising flour

1 tablespoon ground almonds

2 tablespoons milk

For the icing

8 oz (225 g) icing sugar

juice of 1 lemon

2 extra pieces of preserved stem ginger in syrup

You will also need a cake tin, 6 x 10 inches (15 x 25.5 cm), 1 inch (2.5 cm) deep, and some baking parchment, 10 x 14 inches (25.5 x 35.5 cm).

Pre-heat the oven to gas mark 3, 325°F (170°C).

In all my years of cooking, this is, quite simply, my favourite cake. It's simple but absolute heaven. The spiciness of the ginger within the moist cake, coupled with the sharpness of the lemon icing, is such that it never fails to please all who eat it.

First, prepare the cake tin by greasing it lightly and lining it with the baking parchment: press it into the tin, folding the corners in to make it fit neatly. The paper should come up 1 inch (2.5 cm) above the edge.

To make the cake, take a large mixing bowl and cream the butter and sugar together until light and fluffy. Next, break the eggs into a jug and beat them with a fork until fluffy, then gradually beat them into the mixture, a little at a time, until all the egg is incorporated. Next, fold in the ginger syrup, and molasses – the best way to add the molasses is to lightly grease a tablespoon, then take the tablespoon of molasses and just push it off the spoon with a rubber spatula into the mixture. Now sift the flour and ground ginger on to a plate, then gradually fold these in, about a tablespoon at a time. Next, fold in the almonds, followed by the milk, and lastly, the grated root ginger and pieces of stem ginger. Now spread the cake mixture evenly in the cake tin, then bake on the middle shelf of the oven for 45-50 minutes, or until the cake is risen, springy and firm to touch in the centre. Leave the cake to cool in the tin for 10 minutes, then turn it out on to a wire rack and make sure it is absolutely cold before you attempt to ice it.

For the icing, sift the icing sugar into a bowl and mix with enough of the lemon juice to make the consistency of thick cream – you might not need all the lemon juice. Now spread the icing over the top of the cake, and don't worry if it dribbles down the sides in places, as this looks quite attractive. Cut the remaining ginger into 15 chunks and place these in lines across the cake so that when you cut it you will have 15 squares, each with a piece of ginger in the centre. It's absolute heaven. If you'd like one or two of these cakes tucked away for a rainy day, they freeze beautifully – simply defrost and put the icing on half an hour before serving.

The Ultimate Carrot Cake with Mascarpone, Fromage Frais and Cinnamon Icing

Serves 8

For the cake

7 oz (200 g) carrots, peeled and coarsely grated

4 oz (110 g) pecan nuts

6 oz (175 g) dark brown soft sugar

2 large eggs

5 fl oz (150 ml) sunflower oil

7 oz (200 g) wholemeal self-raising flour

1 tablespoon ground mixed spice

1 teaspoon bicarbonate of soda

grated zest of 1 orange

4 oz (110 g) sultanas

2 oz (50 g) desiccated coconut

For the icing

9 oz (250 g) mascarpone

7 oz (200 g) 8 per cent fat fromage frais

1 heaped teaspoon ground cinnamon

1 rounded tablespoon golden caster sugar

For the syrup glaze

juice of 1 small orange

1 tablespoon lemon juice

3 oz (75 g) dark brown soft sugar

You will also need two 8 inch (20 cm) sponge tins, 1½ inches (4 cm) deep, lightly greased, and bases lined with baking parchment.

Pre-heat the oven to gas mark 6, 400°F (200°C).

I have been making carrot cake for years, and each time it seems to improve with a little tinkering here and there. This one has been unanimously voted the best ever!

First, place all the pecan nuts on a baking sheet and, using a timer, toast them in the oven for 6-8 minutes. When you have toasted the nuts, turn the oven down to gas mark 3, 325°F (170°C) for the cake.

Now chop one half of the nuts roughly for the cake, and the other more finely for the topping later. To make the cake, whisk the sugar, eggs and oil together in a bowl with an electric hand whisk for 2-3 minutes, then check that there is no sugar left undissolved. Now sift the flour, mixed spice and bicarbonate of soda into the bowl, tipping in the bits of bran left in the sieve. Then stir all this in gently, followed by the remaining cake ingredients.

Divide the batter evenly between the prepared tins and bake the cakes on the centre shelf of the oven for 30 minutes. They should be nicely risen, feel firm and springy to the touch when lightly pressed in the centre, and show signs of shrinking away from the sides of the tin. If not, give them another 2-3 minutes and test again.

Meanwhile, make the icing by whisking all the ingredients together in a bowl until light and fluffy. Then cover with clingfilm and chill for 1-2 hours, until you are ready to ice the cakes.

To make the syrup glaze, whisk together the fruit juices and sugar in another bowl and then, when the cakes come out of the oven, stab them all over with a skewer and quickly spoon the syrup evenly over the hot cakes.

Now leave them on one side to cool in their tins, during which time the syrup will be absorbed. Then when the cakes are completely cold, remove them from the tins. Spread one-third of the icing over one of the cakes, place the other on top, then cover the top and sides with the remaining mixture. Scatter the finely chopped toasted pecan nuts over the top just before serving.

Greek Orange and Honey Syrup Cake with Yoghurt and Pistachios
Serves 12

For the cake

2 small oranges
(about 9 oz/250 g in total)

4½ oz (125 g) ground almonds

6 oz (175 g) very soft butter

6 oz (175 g) golden caster sugar

3 large eggs, beaten

9 oz (250 g) semolina

4½ teaspoons baking powder

For the syrup

8 fl oz (225 ml) Greek
mountain honey

1½ inch (4 cm) cinnamon stick

5 tablespoons orange juice

1½ tablespoons lemon juice

For the topping

7 oz (200 g) Greek yoghurt

1½ oz (40 g) unsalted,
shelled pistachio nuts

2 tablespoons Greek
mountain honey

You will also need a 10 inch
(25.5 cm) springform cake tin,
lightly greased, and the base lined
with greased baking parchment.

Pre-heat the oven to gas mark 6,
400°F (200°C).

The sharp acidity of the orange in this cake combines beautifully with the sweetness of the Greek mountain honey. Because the cake is soaked in syrup, you can make it well ahead (it's best left overnight) and just whip it out when you're ready to serve.

First, cut the oranges into chunks, removing the pips. Then tip the whole lot – flesh, pith and zest – into a food processor and whiz it to a thick purée. Now all you do is simply put all the other cake ingredients into a large bowl and, provided the butter is really soft, just go in with an electric hand whisk and whisk everything together until you have a smooth, well-combined mixture. After that, fold in the orange purée, spoon the mixture into the prepared tin and smooth the top with the back of the spoon.

Now place the cake on the centre shelf of the oven and bake it for an initial 10 minutes. Then lower the temperature to gas mark 4, 350°F (180°C) and bake for a further 40-45 minutes, or until it is golden brown, springy in the centre and has shrunk slightly from the sides of the tin.

Meanwhile, make the syrup. To do this, simply combine the honey and 5 tablespoons water with the cinnamon stick in a small saucepan, place it over a gentle heat, bring it up to simmering point and let it simmer gently for about 5 minutes. After that, take the pan off the heat, remove the cinnamon stick and stir in the orange and lemon juices. Leave the cake aside to cool for 5 minutes, then remove it from the tin to a wire rack to cool, with a large plate underneath. Make a few holes all over it with a skewer before pouring the syrup over the top. (It will look like there is far too much, but don't worry, the cake will absorb more than you think, and any that is not absorbed can be poured from the plate back over the cake.) Then, when the cake is absolutely cold, place it on a serving plate, cover it and leave it in a cool place overnight.

Just before serving, spread the top of the cake with the Greek yoghurt, sprinkle over the pistachios, drizzle with the honey and serve, cut into chunky slices.

Traditional Dundee Cake
Serves 10-12

5 oz (150 g) butter,
at room temperature

5 oz (150 g) golden caster sugar

3 large eggs

8 oz (225 g) plain flour, sifted
with 1 teaspoon baking powder

a dessertspoon of milk,
if necessary

6 oz (175 g) currants

6 oz (175 g) sultanas

2 oz (50 g) glacé cherries, rinsed,
dried and cut into halves

2 oz (50 g) mixed whole candied
peel, finely chopped

2 tablespoons ground almonds

grated zest of 1 small orange

grated zest of 1 small lemon

2 oz (50 g) whole blanched
almonds

You will also need a 7 inch (18 cm)
round cake tin, 4 inches (10 cm)
deep, greased, and lined with
baking parchment.

Pre-heat the oven to gas mark 3,
325°F (170°C).

This is a really good fruit cake for those who don't like the heavy, rich sort. It does have an excellent flavour and a light, crumbly texture.

Put the butter and sugar in a mixing bowl and beat with a wooden spoon until light and fluffy – or an electric hand whisk or mixer will do this much more quickly.

Whisk the eggs, then beat them into the creamed butter and sugar, a little at a time (don't worry if the mixture curdles a little). Next, using a large tablespoon, carefully fold in the flour and baking powder. Your mixture needs to be of a good, soft, dropping consistency so, if it seems too dry, add a dessertspoon of milk.

Now carefully fold in the currants, sultanas, cherries, mixed peel, ground almonds and orange and lemon zests. Then spoon the mixture into the prepared cake tin, smoothing it out evenly with the back of the spoon. Next, arrange the whole almonds in circles on top of the mixture, but do this carefully and lightly; if they are pressed in they will sink during the baking. Place the cake on the middle shelf of the oven and bake for 2 hours or until the centre is firm and springy to the touch. Let the cake cool before taking it out of the tin. This cake keeps very well in an airtight tin and tastes all the better if kept for a few days before cutting.

Old-fashioned Cherry Cake
Serves 10-12

9 oz (250 g) glacé cherries, quartered (no need to rinse)

8 oz (225 g) butter, at room temperature

8 oz (225 g) golden caster sugar

4 large eggs, lightly beaten

8 oz (225 g) plain flour

½ teaspoon baking powder

4 oz (110 g) ground almonds

a few drops of almond essence

1 tablespoon milk

2 tablespoons demerara sugar

You will also need an 8 inch (20 cm) round cake tin, 4 inches (10 cm) deep, the base and side lined with baking parchment.

Pre-heat the oven to gas mark 4, 350°F (180°C).

Cherry cake has always been a firm family favourite. However, sometimes without there being any possible explanation, those unobliging cherries refuse to stay suspended in the cake and, sadly, end up in a heap at the bottom! The answer is to use the right recipe – and we've had lots of complimentary letters about this one!

First of all, cream the butter and sugar together until light, pale and fluffy. Now gradually beat in the eggs, a little at a time. Then sift the flour and baking powder together, and carefully fold this into the creamed mixture, using a large metal spoon. Toss the quartered cherries in, together with the ground almonds, and carefully fold these into the cake, adding one or two drops of almond essence and the milk. Now spoon the cake mix into the prepared tin, level off the top with the back of the spoon, then sprinkle with the demerara sugar.

Bake the cake in the centre of the oven for 1 hour, cover with foil and continue cooking for a further 30 minutes, or until the cake has shrunk away from the side of the tin and the centre is springy to the touch. Cool the cake in the tin for 15 minutes before turning it out on to a wire rack to cool. Store in an airtight tin.

Fresh Coconut Layer Cake
Serves 8

For the sponge cake

3 oz (75 g) finely grated fresh coconut

6 oz (175 g) self-raising flour

1 rounded teaspoon baking powder

3 large eggs, at room temperature

6 oz (175 g) very soft butter

6 oz (175 g) golden caster sugar

1 teaspoon pure vanilla extract

For the coconut frosting

1½ oz (40 g) finely grated fresh coconut

9 oz (250 g) mascarpone

7 fl oz (200 ml) fromage frais

1 teaspoon pure vanilla extract

1 dessertspoon golden caster sugar

For the topping and sides

2 oz (50 g) coarsely grated fresh coconut

You will also need two 8 inch (20 cm), sponge tins,1½ inches (4 cm) deep, lightly greased, and the bases lined with baking parchment.

Pre-heat the oven to gas mark 3, 325°F (170°C).

The optimum word here is 'fresh'. If you've ever suffered coconut cakes made only with dry, dull, desiccated coconut, let me transport you to a different world. Fresh coconut (you'll only need one) is very moist and has a fragrant, slightly sour, sweet flesh that is perfect for this cake.

Before you start making the cake, you'll first have to deal with the coconut. Not half as impenetrable as it might seem, as all you do is first push a skewer into the three holes in the top of the coconut and drain out the milk. Then place the coconut in a polythene bag and sit it on a hard surface – a stone floor or an outside paving stone. Then give it a hefty whack with a hammer – it won't be that difficult to break. Now remove the pieces from the bag and, using a cloth to protect your hands, prise the top of a knife between the nut and the shell. You should find that you can force the whole piece out in one go. Now discard the shell and take off the inner skin, using a potato peeler. The coconut is now ready to use. The best way to grate coconut flesh is with the grating disc of a food processor, but a hand grater will do just as well.

To make the cake, sift the flour and baking powder into a large bowl, holding the sieve high to give them a good airing. Now just add all the other ingredients, except the grated coconut, to the bowl and go in with an electric hand whisk and combine everything until you have a smooth mixture, which will take about 1 minute. If you don't have an electric hand whisk, use a wooden spoon, with just a little more effort.

What you should now have is a mixture that drops off a spoon when you give it a tap on the side of the bowl. If it seems a little stiff, add a drop of water and mix again. Finally, stir in the 3 oz (75 g) finely grated coconut and divide the mixture between the tins. Now place them on the centre shelf of the oven for 30-35 minutes. To test whether the cakes are cooked, lightly touch the centre of each with a finger: if it leaves no impression and the sponges spring back, they are ready.

Next, remove them from the oven, then wait about 5 minutes before turning them out on to a wire cooling rack. Gently peel off the base papers and, when the cakes are absolutely cold, carefully divide each one horizontally into two halves, using a very sharp serrated knife.

Now make up the frosting by simply whisking all the ingredients together in a bowl to combine them. Next, select the plate or stand you want to serve the cake on – you'll also need a palette knife for the frosting – then simply place one cake layer on first, followed by a thin layer of frosting (about a fifth), followed by the next layer of cake and frosting, and so on.

After that, use the rest of the frosting to coat the sides and top of the cake. Don't worry how it looks: the good thing is that it's all going to be covered with the rest of the grated coconut next. And that's it!

Very Sticky Prune and Date Cake
Serves 16

6 oz (175 g) ready-to-eat pitted prunes, roughly chopped

8 oz (225 g) pitted dates, roughly chopped

4 oz (110 g) raisins

4 oz (110 g) currants

10 oz (275 g) butter

1 x 397 g tin condensed milk

5 oz (150 g) plain flour

5 oz (150 g) wholemeal flour

a pinch of salt

¾ teaspoon bicarbonate of soda

1 heaped tablespoon chunky marmalade

2 tablespoons apricot jam, to glaze

You will also need an 8 in (20 cm) square cake tin, greased, and lined with baking parchment, plus extra baking parchment to cover the cake.

Pre-heat the oven to gas mark 3, 325°F (170°C).

This is one of the easiest cakes ever, but with a flavour that is really special – dark and caramelised with lots of luscious fruit.

Begin by placing all the fruit in a largeish saucepan (it needs to be large because the mixture splutters a lot), then add the butter, condensed milk and 10 fl oz (275 ml) of water and bring everything up to the boil, stirring frequently with a wooden spoon to prevent the mixture sticking. Now turn the heat down to low and simmer for exactly 3 minutes, stirring now and then. Don't worry about the appalling look of what will be a very sloppy mixture; this is quite normal. After 3 minutes, transfer the mixture to a large mixing bowl and let it cool down for about 30 minutes. While it's cooling, weigh out the flours and sift them into a bowl with a pinch of salt and the bicarbonate of soda (when sieving wholemeal flour you frequently find small quantities of bran left in the sieve: these can be tipped on to the already-sieved flour).

When the fruit mixture has cooled, stir in the flour, salt and bicarbonate of soda, using a large metal spoon, then add the marmalade. Now spoon the mixture into the prepared tin and, because this cake does get rather brown on top if not protected, you should cover it with a double square of baking parchment with a hole the size of a 50p piece in the centre. Then pop it on to the centre shelf of the oven and bake for 2-2¼ hours. Have a look after 2 hours – the cake is cooked if the centre feels springy when lightly pressed.

After removing the cake from the oven, let it cool in the tin for 10 minutes before turning out on to a wire rack. Then, when the cake is completely cold, gently heat the apricot jam in a small saucepan with 1 tablespoon of water, until all the lumps of jam have dissolved. Now sieve the jam to remove any pieces of fruit, then brush the glaze all over the top of the cake to make it lovely and shiny.

This is quite a large cake that will keep well for several weeks in an airtight tin and even improves, I think, with keeping. If you prefer, you could make this in two 1 lb (450 g) loaf tins and halve the cooking time.

Polenta and Ricotta Cake
with Dates and Pecans
Serves 8-10

7 oz (200 g) polenta

9 oz (250 g) ricotta

6 oz (175 g) chopped dates

2 oz (50 g) pecan nuts, roughly chopped

3 tablespoons Amaretto

7 oz (200 g) self-raising flour

1 rounded teaspoon baking powder

1 heaped teaspoon ground cinnamon

8 oz (225 g) golden caster sugar

4 oz (110 g) butter, melted

1 tablespoon demerara sugar

You will also need an 8 inch (20 cm) springform cake tin, lightly greased, and lined with baking parchment.

Pre-heat the oven to gas mark 3, 325°F (170°C).

This is a very unusual cake, quite different in flavour and texture from anything else. It's Italian in origin and polenta (cornmeal) gives it a sandy texture, while at the same time ricotta cheese and Amaretto liqueur give a wonderful moistness. It also freezes very well, but, as you won't have any left over, you might as well make two – it's so dead easy!

First of all, place the dates in a small bowl, pour the Amaretto over them and leave them to soak for 15 minutes. Then place the pecans on a baking tray and toast them for 6-8 minutes – use a timer so they don't get over-cooked. Now, to make the cake, take a large mixing bowl and first sift the polenta, flour, baking powder and cinnamon. Keep the sieve held high to give the flour a good airing, then tip the grains from the polenta in to join the rest.

Next, add the caster sugar, ricotta, melted butter and 7 fl oz (200 ml) of tepid water and whisk with an electric hand whisk until everything is thoroughly blended (about 1 minute). After that, fold in the nuts, dates and the liqueur in which they were soaking. Fold everything in thoroughly, spoon the mixture into the prepared tin and smooth the top with the back of a spoon. Now scatter the demerara sugar evenly over the surface, then pop the cake into a pre-heated oven on the middle shelf, where it will take between 1¾ and 2 hours to cook. When it's cooked, it will feel springy in the centre when you make a very light depression with your little finger. If it's not cooked, give it another 10 minutes and then do another test.

When the cake is ready, remove it from the oven, allow it to cool in the tin for 15 minutes, then remove it from the tin and leave it to cool completely on a wire rack. Store in an airtight tin.

Honey and Spice Cake
Makes 15 squares

For the cake

3 oz (75 g) clear, runny honey

1 teaspoon ground ginger

1 teaspoon ground cinnamon

¼ teaspoon ground cloves

8 oz (225 g) plain flour

3 oz (75 g) golden caster sugar

finely grated zest of 1 small orange

finely grated zest of 1 small lemon

4 oz (110 g) butter,
at room temperature

1 large egg, beaten

1 teaspoon bicarbonate of soda

2 oz (50 g) mixed whole candied
peel, finely chopped

For the icing and decoration

6 oz (175 g) icing sugar

1 tablespoon lemon juice

6 pieces of crystallised ginger,
chopped into 15

You will also need a 7 inch (18 cm)
square cake tin (or 8 inch/20 cm
round tin, 4 inches/10 cm deep),
lightly buttered, and lined with
baking parchment.

Pre-heat the oven to gas mark 3,
325°F (170°C).

This cake has a tangy citrus flavour and tastes sensational with a sharp lemon icing. It is also nice just dusted with icing sugar.

First of all, weigh a cup or small basin on the scales, then weigh the 3 oz (75 g) of honey into it. Now place the cup or basin into a saucepan containing barely simmering water and warm the honey a little, but be careful: it mustn't be too hot, just warm.

Next, sift the flour and spices into a large mixing bowl, then add the sugar and the orange and lemon zests. Now add the butter in small pieces, then rub it lightly into the flour, using your fingertips, until the mixture becomes crumbly. Next, lightly mix in the beaten egg, using a large fork, followed by the warm honey. Then in a small basin, mix the bicarbonate of soda with 3 tablespoons of cold water, stir until dissolved, then add it to the cake mixture and beat, quite hard, until the mixture is smooth and soft. Finally, stir in the mixed peel and spoon the mixture into the prepared tin, spreading it out evenly.

Bake the cake just above the centre of the oven for about 50 minutes or until well risen and springy to the touch. Cool it for 10 minutes, then turn it out on to a wire rack to get quite cold.

Meanwhile, prepare the icing by sifting the icing sugar into a bowl, then add a tablespoon of warm water, along with the lemon juice, and mix to a thin consistency that will coat the back of a spoon. Now place the cake on a wire rack, with a large plate underneath, and pour the icing all over, letting it run down and coat the sides a bit. Then decorate the top in lines with the chopped ginger. Cut into 15 pieces and store the cake in an airtight container.

Blueberry and Cinnamon Muffin
Cake with Streusel Topping

Blueberry and Cinnamon Muffin Cake with Streusel Topping
Serves 8-10

For the cake

10 oz (275 g) blueberries

½ teaspoon ground cinnamon

10 oz (275 g) plain flour

1 tablespoon baking powder

½ teaspoon salt

2 medium eggs

3 oz (75 g) golden caster sugar

6 fl oz (175 ml) milk

4 oz (110 g) butter

For the topping

3 oz (75 g) self-raising flour

1 teaspoon ground cinnamon

1 oz (25 g) butter,
at room temperature

3 oz (75 g) demerara sugar

2 oz (50 g) chopped toasted
hazelnuts

You will also need a 9 inch
(23 cm) springform cake tin,
lightly greased, and the base lined
with baking parchment.

Pre-heat the oven to gas mark 5,
375°F (190°C).

I still get letters from people saying they can't make muffins. My message to them is don't try too hard – undermixing is the golden rule and, once mastered, the American muffin mix makes the lightest cakes in the world. Having got totally hooked on making muffins, I realised that the muffin mixture could be baked in an ordinary cake tin and served, cut into thick slices – either as a dessert fresh and still warm from the oven and topped with Greek yoghurt, or as a cake for tea in the garden on a sunny day.

As with all muffins, you need to sift the dry ingredients twice, so place the flour, baking powder, salt and cinnamon in a sieve and sift them into a bowl. In another large mixing bowl, whisk the eggs, sugar and milk together, then melt the butter and pour this into the egg mixture, whisking once again.

Now sift the flour mixture in on top of the egg mixture and fold it in, using as few folds as possible (ignore the lumpy appearance at this stage and don't be tempted to overmix). Fold in the blueberries and spoon into the tin.

To make the topping, you can use the same bowl that the flour was in. Add the flour, cinnamon and butter and rub the butter in until crumbly, then add the sugar and hazelnuts and mix well. Finally, sprinkle in 1 tablespoon of cold water, then press the mixture loosely together. Now sprinkle this mixture all over the cake.

Bake on the centre shelf of the oven for 1¼ hours or until it feels springy in the centre. Allow it to cool in the tin for 30 minutes before removing the sides of the tin. Then slide a palette knife gently under the base and transfer the cake to a wire rack to finish cooling.

A Classic Sponge Cake
(with Passion-fruit Filling)
Serves 8

For the sponge cake

6 oz (175 g) self-raising flour

1 rounded teaspoon baking powder

3 large eggs, at room temperature

6 oz (175 g) very soft butter

6 oz (175 g) golden caster sugar

½ teaspoon pure vanilla extract

a little sifted icing sugar
for dusting

For the filling

6 passion fruit

9 oz (250 g) mascarpone

7 fl oz (200 ml) fromage frais

1 dessertspoon golden
caster sugar

1 teaspoon pure vanilla extract

You will also need two 8 inch
(20 cm) sponge tins, 1½ inches
(4 cm) deep, lightly greased, and the
bases lined with baking parchment.

Pre-heat the oven to gas mark 3,
325°F (170°C).

This sponge cake could also be made in a 7 inch (18 cm) tin (just use 2 eggs and 4 oz/110 g each of flour, sugar and butter), and filled with jam and cream. And, while the soft fruits of summer, when they're available, are perfect for filling sponge cakes, in winter, passion fruit fulfil all the criteria needed – something sharp, fragrant and acidic to contrast with the richness of the cake and cream.

Take a very large mixing bowl, put the flour and baking powder in a sieve and sift them into the bowl, holding the sieve high to give it a good airing as it goes down. Now all you do is simply add all the other cake ingredients (except the icing sugar) to the bowl and, provided the butter is really soft, just go in with an electric hand whisk and whisk everything together until you have a smooth, well-combined mixture, which will take about 1 minute. If you don't have an electric hand whisk, you can use a wooden spoon, with just a little bit more effort. What you will now end up with is a mixture that drops off a spoon when you give it a tap on the side of the bowl. If it seems a little too stiff, add a little water and mix again.

Now divide the mixture between the two tins, level it out and place the tins on the centre shelf of the oven. The cakes will take 30-35 minutes to cook, but don't open the oven door until 30 minutes have elapsed. To test whether the cakes are cooked or not, touch the centre of each lightly with a finger: if it leaves no impression and the sponges spring back, they are ready.

Next, remove them from the oven, then wait about 5 minutes before turning them out on to a wire cooling rack. Carefully peel off the base papers, which is easier if you make a little fold at the edge of the paper first, then pull the paper gently away without trying to lift it off. Now leave the sponges to get completely cold, then add the filling.

To make this, first slice the passion fruit into halves and, using a teaspoon, scoop all the flesh, juice and seeds into a bowl. Next, in another bowl, combine the mascarpone, fromage frais, sugar and vanilla extract, using a balloon whisk, which is the quickest way to blend them all together. After that, fold in about two-thirds of the passion fruit. Now place the first sponge cake on the plate or cake stand you are going to serve it on, then spread half the filling over it, drizzle the rest of the passion fruit over that, then spread the remaining filling over the passion fruit.

Lastly, place the other cake on top, press it gently so that the filling oozes out at the edges, then dust the surface with a little sifted icing sugar.

Iced Lemon Curd Layer Cake
Serves 6

For the sponge cake

grated zest of 1 lemon

1 tablespoon lemon juice

6 oz (175 g) self-raising flour,
sifted with 1 teaspoon
baking powder

6 oz (175 g) butter,
at room temperature

6 oz (175 g) golden caster sugar

3 large eggs

For the lemon curd

3 oz (75 g) golden caster sugar

grated zest and juice of 1 large
juicy lemon

2 large eggs

2 oz (50 g) unsalted butter

For the icing

zest of 1 large lemon

2 oz (50 g) sifted icing sugar

2-3 teaspoons lemon juice

You will also need two 7 inch (18 cm),
sponge tins, 1½ inches (4 cm) deep,
lightly greased, the bases lined
with baking parchment, and
the parchment then greased.

Pre-heat the oven to gas mark 3,
325°F (170°C).

You couldn't get a more lemony recipe than this: layers of lemon-flavoured sponge, filled with home-made lemon curd and then a lemon icing for the finishing touch. It's wonderful.

Just measure all the cake ingredients into a mixing bowl and beat – ideally, with an electric hand whisk – till you have a smooth, creamy consistency. Then divide the mixture evenly between the two tins and bake them on the centre shelf of the oven for about 35 minutes or until the centres feel springy when lightly touched with a little finger.

While the cakes are cooking, make the lemon curd. Place the sugar and grated lemon zest in a bowl, whisk the lemon juice together with the eggs, then pour this over the sugar. Then add the butter cut into little pieces, and place the bowl over a pan of barely simmering water. Stir frequently till thickened – about 20 minutes. You don't have to stay with it – just come back from time to time to give it a stir.

When the cakes are cooked, remove them from the oven and, after about 5 minutes, turn them out on to a wire rack and peel off the base papers. When they are absolutely cold – and not before – carefully cut each cake horizontally into two, using a sharp serrated knife. Now spread the curd thickly to sandwich the sponges together.

Then, to make the icing, begin by removing the zest from the lemon – it's best to use a zester to get long, curly strips. Then sift the icing sugar into a bowl and gradually stir in the lemon juice until you have a soft, runny consistency. Allow the icing to stand for 5 minutes before spreading it on top of the cake with a knife, almost to the edges, and don't worry if it runs a little down the sides of the cake. Then scatter the lemon zest over the top and leave it for half an hour for the icing to firm up before serving.

Austrian Coffee and Walnut Cake with Coffee Cream
Serves 8

For the sponge cake

1½ tablespoons instant coffee, mixed with 2 tablespoons boiling water

3 oz (75 g) walnut halves

6 oz (175 g) self-raising flour

1½ teaspoons baking powder

6 oz (175 g) very soft butter

6 oz (175 g) golden caster sugar

3 large eggs, at room temperature

For the syrup

1 tablespoon instant espresso coffee powder

2 oz (50 g) demerara sugar

For the filling and topping

1 tablespoon instant espresso coffee powder

9 oz (250 g) mascarpone

7 fl oz (200 ml) 8 per cent fat fromage frais

1 rounded tablespoon golden caster sugar

walnut halves, reserved from the cake

You will also need two 8 inch (20 cm), sponge tins, 1½ inches (4 cm) deep, lightly greased, and the bases lined with baking parchment.

Pre-heat the oven to gas mark 3, 325°F (170°C).

This is unashamedly rich and luscious. Firstly, coffee and walnuts have a great affinity; secondly, so do coffee and creaminess; and thirdly, because the cake is soaked in coffee syrup, it's also meltingly moist.

First of all, you need to toast all the walnuts, so spread them on a baking sheet and place in the pre-heated oven for 7-8 minutes. After that, reserve 9 or 10 halves to use as decoration later and finely chop the rest. Take a very large mixing bowl, put the flour and baking powder in a sieve and sift them into the bowl, holding the sieve high to give everything a good airing as it goes down.

Now all you do is simply add the other cake ingredients (except the coffee and walnuts) to the bowl and, provided the butter is really soft, just go in with an electric hand whisk and whisk everything together until you have a smooth, well-combined mixture, then fold in the coffee and chopped walnuts. This will take about 1 minute but, if you don't have an electric hand whisk, you can use a wooden spoon and just a little bit more effort. What you should end up with is a soft mixture that drops off the spoon easily when you give it a sharp tap; if not, add a spot of water.

Divide the mixture between the prepared sponge tins, spreading the mixture around evenly. Then place the tins on the centre shelf of the oven and bake them for 30 minutes. While the cakes are cooking, you can make up the syrup and the filling and topping. For the syrup, first place the coffee and sugar in a heatproof jug, then measure 2 fl oz (55 ml) boiling water into it and stir briskly until the coffee and sugar have dissolved, which will take about 1 minute. Next, the filling and topping, and all you do here is place all the ingredients, except the reserved walnuts, in a bowl and whisk them together till thoroughly blended. Then cover the bowl with clingfilm and chill till needed.

When the cakes are cooked, ie, feel springy in the centre, remove them from the oven but leave them in their tins and prick them all over with a skewer while they are still hot. Now spoon the syrup as evenly as possible over each one and leave them to soak up the liquid as they cool in their tins. When they are absolutely cold, turn them out very carefully and peel off the base papers – I like to turn one out on to the plate you're going to serve it on. Then spread half the filling and topping mixture over the first cake, place the other cake carefully on top and spread the other half over.

Finally, arrange the reserved walnut halves in a circle all around. It's a good idea to chill the cake if you're not going to serve it immediately.

Moist Chocolate and Almond Cake

Moist Chocolate and Almond Cake
Serves 8-10

For the cake

4 oz (110 g) dark chocolate
(70-75 per cent cocoa solids),
grated

4 oz (110 g) ground almonds

4 oz (110 g) butter,
at room temperature

6 oz (175 g) golden caster sugar

4 large eggs, separated

6 tablespoons milk

6 oz (175 g) self-raising flour,
sifted

To decorate

6 oz (175 g) dark chocolate
(70-75 per cent cocoa solids),
broken up

1 rounded tablespoon
crème fraîche

toasted flaked almonds

You will also need an 8 inch
(20 cm) round cake tin, greased,
and lined with baking parchment.

Pre-heat the oven to gas mark 7,
425°F (220°C).

This is a beautifully moist cake, light in colour, but with dark speckles of melted chocolate in it.

Start by creaming the butter and sugar together until they're light, pale and fluffy. Beat the egg yolks thoroughly together and add them to the mixture, about a teaspoonful at a time, beating well after each addition. When all the yolks are in, lightly fold in the ground almonds, grated chocolate and milk, using a metal spoon.

Now, in a separate, dry, clean bowl, whisk the egg whites till they reach the soft peak stage, and then fold them into the rest of the mixture gently and carefully so as not to lose all the air you have whisked in. Finally, add the flour – again, folding that in carefully with a metal spoon.

Next, spoon the mixture into the prepared tin, level it off, place it on the centre shelf in the oven, reduce the heat to gas mark 3, 325°F (170°C) and bake the cake for 1 hour 10 minutes to 1 hour 15 minutes or until the centre is springy when lightly touched. Allow the cake to stand in the tin for 5 minutes, then turn it out on to a wire rack to cool.

To decorate, melt the 6 oz (175 g) of dark chocolate in a heatproof bowl, which should be sitting over a saucepan of barely simmering water, making sure the bottom of the bowl doesn't touch the water. The chocolate should take about 5 minutes to become smooth and glossy. Allow it to cool for 2-3 minutes and thicken slightly and then stir the crème fraîche into the chocolate.

Split the cake in half and use half the chocolate to sandwich it together, and the other half to spread over the top, making patterns with a knife. Decorate with toasted almonds and store in an airtight tin till needed.

Easter Simnel Cake
Serves 12

For the cake

4 oz (110 g) whole blanched almonds

1 lb 2 oz (500 g) block of golden marzipan

8 oz (225 g) plain flour

1 tablespoon baking powder

1 rounded teaspoon ground mixed spice

5 oz (150 g) light brown soft sugar

5 oz (150 g) butter, well softened

2 tablespoons milk

3 large eggs, beaten

14 oz (400 g) mincemeat

12 oz (350 g) mixed dried fruit

2 oz (50 g) mixed whole candied peel, chopped

grated zests of 1 orange and 1 lemon

To decorate

icing sugar for dusting

9 oz (250 g) ready-to-roll icing

1 dessertspoon redcurrant jelly

marzipan (reserved from the cake)

1 egg yolk, beaten

You will also need a deep, round cake tin, 8 inches (20 cm) in diameter, the base and sides lined with a double layer of baking parchment.

Pre-heat the oven to gas mark 6, 400°F (200°C).

Simnel Cake was not originally baked at Easter but on Mothering Sunday, as a kind of mid-Lent treat. Somehow or other, it got postponed until the great feast of Easter itself – which, in my book, is precisely where it deserves to be, since it makes the perfect family treat for a bank holiday weekend. This version is baked with chunks of marzipan interspersed in the cake mixture, which melt deliciously into the fruit.

You need to begin by toasting the almonds to give them some extra crunch and flavour. So spread them out on a baking sheet and pop them in the pre-heated oven for 8-10 minutes. Don't guess the time, please use a timer – they need to be lightly toasted to a golden brown colour and you could end up with an expensive mistake if you try and guess!

Now remove the almonds and reduce the oven temperature to gas mark 2, 300°F (150°C). Then, when the almonds are cool, chop them roughly. Next, unwrap the marzipan, cut the block into two halves, re-wrap one of them for use later, and chop the remaining half into ½ inch (1 cm) cubes. Toss them in 1 tablespoon of the flour for the cake.

For the cake, take your largest mixing bowl, sift the flour, baking powder and spice in, then simply place all the ingredients for the cake, except the marzipan, into the bowl. Then take an electric hand whisk for preference or, failing that, a wooden spoon, and give everything a really good mixing – which will take about 2-3 minutes – to get it all perfectly and evenly distributed. Finally, gently fold in the squares of marzipan and any remaining flour.

Now, using a rubber spatula, spoon the mixture into the prepared tin, levelling the surface with the back of the spatula. Place a suitably sized square of double baking parchment with a hole the size of a 50p piece in the centre over the top. Place the cake on the centre shelf of the oven and bake for 2¾-3 hours. Have a look after 2¾ hours – the cake is cooked if the centre feels springy when lightly pressed. When it is cooked, leave it in the tin for 30 minutes before turning it out on to a wire rack to cool.

For the decoration, first dust a work surface with icing sugar and roll out the icing to the same size as the top of the cake (you can use the base of the tin as a guide here). Then brush the top of the cake with redcurrant jelly and fit the icing on top of the cake, pressing it securely all round and using a rolling pin to level it as much as possible. Trim off any overhanging pieces. Roll out the reserved marzipan to a rectangle about 6 x 9 inches (15 x 23 cm), then cut it into 12 long strips about ½ inch (1 cm) wide for the lattice topping. Assembling the lattice goes as follows: first lay half the strips across the cake, leaving about ¾ inch (2 cm) gap between each strip. Then begin to thread the rest of the strips, one at a time, under and over the first ones, going at right angles. Finally, use some scissors to snip the overhanging marzipan away and press firmly all round to make the edges as neat as possible.

Now pre-heat the grill and, when it's really hot (it will take at least 10 minutes to come up to full blast), brush the marzipan strips with the egg yolk and place the cake under the grill, about 4 inches (10 cm) from the heat. Give it about 30 seconds, watching it like a hawk, until it turns a toasted brown colour. The cake is now ready to serve or be stored. It looks very pretty if you tie a ribbon round the circumference and decorate with some Easter flowers.

Spiced Apple Muffin Cake with Pecan Streusel Topping
Serves 10-12

For the cake

12 oz (350 g) Bramley cooking apples (weight after peeling and coring), chopped into ½ inch (1 cm) cubes

1 heaped teaspoon ground cinnamon

1 teaspoon ground cloves

½ whole nutmeg, grated

4 oz (110 g) butter

10 oz (275 g) plain flour

1 tablespoon baking powder, plus 1 teaspoon

½ teaspoon salt

2 large eggs, at room temperature

3 oz (75 g) golden caster sugar

6 fl oz (175 ml) milk

For the topping

3 oz (75 g) self-raising flour

3 oz (75 g) demerara sugar

1 rounded teaspoon ground cinnamon

1 oz (25 g) soft butter

2 oz (50 g) pecan nuts, roughly chopped

You will also need a 9 inch (23 cm) springform cake tin, lightly greased, and the base lined with baking parchment.

Pre-heat the oven to gas mark 5, 375°F (190°C).

In the summer, you could always replace the apples with 12 oz (350 g) of fresh apricots, stoned and chopped, or, in the autumn, with 12 oz (350 g) of plums, stoned and chopped. In both cases, though, weigh after stoning. This recipe will also make 24 mini or 12 large muffins, cooking them for 20 and 30 minutes respectively.

First of all, place the butter in a small saucepan and put it on a gentle heat to melt. Then, as with all muffin mixtures, you need to sift the dry ingredients twice, so place the flour, all the baking powder, salt, cinnamon, cloves and grated nutmeg in a sieve and sift them into a bowl.

Then, in another large mixing bowl, whisk the eggs, sugar and milk together, pour the melted butter into the egg mixture and give it all another good whisk. Now sift the flour mixture again straight in on top of the egg mixture and fold it in, making as few folds as possible. Ignore the horrible lumpy mixture you're now faced with and don't be tempted to overmix. I think this is where people go wrong: they can't believe that what looks like a disaster can possibly turn into something so light and luscious. Now fold in the chopped apple and then spoon the whole lot into the tin, levelling off the surface.

Next, make the topping, and you can use the same bowl. Just add the flour, sugar and cinnamon and rub the butter in with your fingertips until crumbly. Finally, sprinkle in the nuts and 1 tablespoon cold water, then press the mixture loosely together. Again, it will be quite lumpy – no problem! Now spoon the topping over the surface of the cake, then bake on the centre shelf of the oven for about 1¼ hours, until it feels springy in the centre. Allow the cake to cool in the tin for 30 minutes before removing the sides, then gently slide a palette knife under the base and transfer the cake to a wire rack to finish cooling. Serve this as fresh as possible, either on its own, or warm as a dessert with whipped cream, crème fraîche or vanilla ice cream.

Irish Whiskey Christmas Cakes

Makes four 4 inch (10 cm) square cakes

For the pre-soaking

10 fl oz (275 ml) Irish whiskey

1½ teaspoons Angostura bitters

4 oz (110 g) pitted, ready-to-eat prunes

2 oz (50 g) glacé cherries

2 oz (50 g) whole unblanched almonds

4 oz (110 g) mixed whole candied peel, finely diced

1 lb (450 g) raisins

8 oz (225 g) currants

½ rounded teaspoon ground cinnamon

½ teaspoon freshly grated nutmeg

½ teaspoon ground cloves

1½ teaspoons pure vanilla extract

1 tablespoon molasses sugar

grated zest of 1 orange

grated zest of 1 lemon

½ teaspoon salt

For the cake

9 oz (250 g) self-raising flour, sifted

9 oz (250 g) demerara sugar

9 oz (250 g) very soft, unsalted butter

5 large eggs, at room temperature

If you've never made a Christmas cake before, these are dead easy, and you won't be disappointed. I prefer the much thinner layer of marzipan and icing, and the flavour of the Irish whiskey in the icing, as well as the cakes, is brilliant. To keep them for any length of time, let the marzipan dry out (covered with a clean tea cloth) for a week before icing. If you prefer, you can keep the cake whole and decorate it as an 8 inch (20 cm) cake.

One week before you intend to bake the cake, measure out the whiskey, bitters and 3 tablespoons of water into a large saucepan, then roughly chop the prunes, cherries and almonds. Add these, along with the rest of the pre-soaking ingredients, to the pan, ticking them as you go to make sure nothing gets left out. Now stir and bring the mixture up to simmering point, then, keeping the heat low, simmer very gently, without a lid, for 15 minutes. After that, allow everything to cool completely, then pour the mixture into a large jar with a lid or an airtight plastic container and leave it in the fridge for 7 days, giving it a little shake from time to time.

When you're ready to bake the cake, pre-heat the oven to gas mark 1, 275°F (140°C). All you need to do is measure out the flour, sugar and butter into a very large bowl, then add the eggs and either whisk, or beat with a wooden spoon, until everything is evenly blended. Now gradually fold in the fruit mixture until it is evenly distributed. Then spoon the mixture into the prepared tin, levelling the surface with the back of the spoon. Bake in the centre of the oven for 3 hours without opening the door, then cover the cake with a double thickness of baking parchment and continue to bake it for a further 30 minutes or until the centre feels springy when lightly touched. Cool the cake for 45 minutes in the tin, then remove it to a wire rack. When it's completely cold, wrap it in a double layer of baking parchment, then foil, and store it in an airtight container.

To decorate the cakes, take a sharp knife and cut the cake into quarters so you end up with four 4 inch (10 cm) square cakes. Then melt the jam with the whiskey in a small saucepan and stir it a few times until all the lumps have dissolved. Now, using a brush, coat the surface of each cake quite generously with it. Take the marzipan and cut

For the marzipan

1 heaped tablespoon apricot jam

1 tablespoon Irish whiskey

1 lb 2 oz (500 g) block of marzipan

a little unrefined golden icing sugar for dusting

For the icing

1 large egg white

1 dessertspoon molasses syrup (or black treacle)

1 lb 4 oz (570 g) unrefined golden icing sugar, sieved

2½ tablespoons Irish whiskey

You will also need an 8 inch (20 cm) square cake tin, greased, the base and sides lined with a double thickness of baking parchment to sit 4 inches (10 cm) deep, plus some extra baking parchment to cover the cake.

To finish the cakes, you will need 4 lengths of ribbon 4 ft (1.2 m) long, 1½ inches (4 cm) wide.

off a quarter of the block, then, on a surface lightly dusted with icing sugar, roll the piece into an 8 inch (20 cm) square. Now, with a sharp knife, cut the square into quarters so you end up with four 4 inch (10 cm) square pieces. Gently take each square and place one on top of each cake, lightly pressing the marzipan down. Next, cut the remaining piece of marzipan in half and roll each half into a strip measuring 6 x 16 inches (15 x 40 cm), then cut each strip in half lengthways so you are left with 4 strips: one for the sides of each cake. Press each strip lightly around the edges of each cake and pinch to seal at the join with the top piece of marzipan.

For the icing, place the egg white and molasses in a large bowl and, using an electric hand whisk, whisk together thoroughly. Now, with the whisk running, add a tablespoon of icing sugar at a time and keep adding it until the mixture thickens. As it begins to crumble, add a tablespoon of the whiskey to combine the mixture, then carry on adding more icing sugar until it thickens. Add another tablespoon of whiskey, then the rest of the icing sugar and whiskey, and keep whisking until everything is blended together. Divide the icing into four. Using a palette knife, smooth icing over the top and sides of your cakes, dipping the knife into a small saucepan of simmering water to make it easier to spread. To finish, dip the knife in the simmering water once more and make swirls with the knife over the surface, then leave the cakes to dry overnight. Wrap each cake in parchment, then in foil, and keep in an airtight container. To finish, tie a length of ribbon around each one.

Coconut Lime Cake
Serves 8

For the sponge cake

2 oz (50 g) desiccated coconut

2 limes

6 oz (175 g) self-raising flour

6 oz (175 g) golden caster sugar

6 oz (175 g) very soft butter

3 large eggs, lightly beaten

2 tablespoons dried coconut milk powder

1 rounded teaspoon baking powder

For the icing

3 limes

8 oz (225 g) icing sugar

You will also need two 8 inch (20 cm), sponge tins, 1½ inches (4 cm) deep, and the bases lined with baking parchment.

Pre-heat the oven to gas mark 3, 325°F (170°C).

This superb cake underlines what a perfect combination of flavours coconut makes with lime.

For the cake, start off by grating the zest of the 2 limes on to a small saucer, then cover that with clingfilm and set on one side. Next, measure the desiccated coconut into a small bowl, then squeeze the juice of the limes and pour this over the coconut to allow it to soften and soak up the juice for an hour or so. To make the cake, just take a large, roomy bowl and sift in the flour, lifting the sieve up high to give the flour a good airing. Then simply throw in all the other cake ingredients, including the lime zest and soaked desiccated coconut and, with an electric hand whisk switched to high speed, whisk everything till thoroughly blended – about 2-3 minutes. Now divide the mixture equally between the two prepared tins, smooth to level off the tops and bake on a middle shelf of the oven for 30-35 minutes, or until the centres feel springy to the touch. Allow the cakes to cool in the tins for 5 minutes, then turn them out on to a wire rack to cool completely, carefully peeling off the base papers. They must be completely cold before the icing goes on.

To make the icing, begin by removing the zest from the 3 limes – this is best done with a zester, as you need long, thin, curly strips that look pretty. Then, with your sharpest knife, remove all the outer pith from the limes, then carefully remove each segment (holding the limes over a bowl to catch any juice), sliding the knife in between the membrane so that you have the flesh of the segments only. This is much easier to do with limes than it is with other citrus fruits. Drop the segments into the bowl and squeeze the last drops of juice from the pith. Now sift the icing sugar in on top of the lime segments, a little at a time, carefully folding it in with a tablespoon in order not to break up the lime segments too much. When all the sugar is incorporated, allow the mixture to stand for 5 minutes, then spread half of it on to the surface of one of the cakes and scatter with half the lime zest. Place the other cake on top, spread the rest of the icing on top of that and scatter the rest of the zest over. Then place the cake in the fridge for 30 minutes to firm up the icing before serving.

Tea Breads Loaves

Sticky Gingerbread
Makes 9 squares

1½ teaspoons ground ginger

12 oz (350 g) plain flour

2 teaspoons ground cinnamon

⅛ whole nutmeg, freshly grated

¼ teaspoon white pepper

1 teaspoon bicarbonate of soda

4 tablespoons milk

6 oz (175 g) black treacle

6 oz (175 g) golden syrup

6 oz (175 g) dark brown soft sugar

6 oz (175 g) butter

2 large eggs, lightly beaten

You will also need an 8 inch
(20 cm) square tin with a fixed
base, 2½ inches (6 cm)
deep, buttered, and lined with
baking parchment.

Pre-heat the oven to gas mark 3,
325°F (170°C).

To measure the treacle and syrup for this recipe, warm both slightly to make them easier to handle, then measure them in a glass measuring jug.

First of all, sift the flour and spices, including the pepper, into a large bowl, then mix the bicarbonate of soda with the milk and set on one side. Now place the black treacle, golden syrup, sugar and butter in a saucepan with 5 fl oz (150 ml) water, heat and gently stir until thoroughly melted and blended, but do not let it come anywhere near the boil.

Next, add the syrup mixture to the flour and spices, beating vigorously with a wooden spoon; when the mixture is smooth, beat in the eggs, a little at a time, followed by the bicarbonate of soda and milk. Pour the mixture into the prepared tin and bake for 1¼-1½ hours until well risen, firm to the touch and shrunk away slightly from the sides of the tin.

Remove the cake from the oven and allow to cool in the tin for 5 minutes before turning out. If possible, leave the cake in a cake tin for 24 hours before eating, and serve in thick slices spread with butter.

Spiced Date and Walnut Loaf
Serves 8

4 oz (110 g) pitted dates

2 oz (50 g) walnuts

4 oz (110 g) butter

2 oz (50 g) black treacle

6 oz (175 g) golden syrup

5 fl oz (150 ml) milk

2 large eggs

8 oz (225 g) plain flour

1 teaspoon ground mixed spice

2 teaspoons ground ginger

1 teaspoon bicarbonate of soda

You will also need a 2 lb (900 g)
loaf tin, lightly greased.

Pre-heat the oven to gas mark 2,
300°F (150°C).

I have to admit I had three attempts at this cake before I got exactly what I wanted – a dark, rather sticky Date and Walnut Loaf – and I think you'll agree that this one is just right.

First, prepare the dates and walnuts. The nuts should be chopped fairly small and the dates individually chopped into fairly small pieces. If you try to chop them all together they tend to stick and it's hard to separate the pieces out.

Now, to make the cake mixture, place the butter, black treacle and syrup in a medium saucepan and melt them together over a gentle heat. Then remove the mixture from the heat, let it cool for a few minutes, and mix the milk into it. Now beat the eggs and add those to the syrup mixture as well.

Next, sift the flour, spices and bicarbonate of soda into a large bowl, holding the sieve up high to give the flour a good airing. Now, with the back of a spoon, make a well in the centre and pour the syrup mixture into it. Then, using an electric hand whisk on a slow speed, begin to whisk the syrup into the dry ingredients, bit by bit, until you have a smooth batter. Then lightly fold in the walnuts and about two-thirds of the dates, and pour the mixture into the prepared tin. Now lightly drop the rest of the dates on the top, pushing them gently in with a skewer. I find adding this amount of dates last of all gives a better distribution, as the mixture is a fairly slack one.

Place the cake on the centre shelf of the oven and bake it for 1½ hours, by which time it will have a very rounded, slightly cracked top. Cool it in the tin for about half an hour before turning it out. Then, when it's absolutely cold, keep it in an airtight container. This is a cake that does seem to improve if kept a couple of days before eating.

Irish Tea Bread
Makes 2 loaves (each serves 4-6)

8 oz (225 g) raisins

8 oz (225 g) currants

8 oz (225 g) sultanas

4 oz (110 g) mixed whole candied peel, cut into ¼ inch (5 mm) pieces

8 oz (225 g) demerara sugar

10 fl oz (275 ml) Lapsang Souchong, Earl Grey or any other hot tea

4 oz (110 g) pecan nuts

1 large egg, at room temperature, lightly beaten with 2 tablespoons milk

1 lb (450 g) self-raising flour

You will also need two 1 lb (450 g) loaf tins, bases lined with baking parchment.

It's always hard for me to believe that this simple little fruit loaf can taste so good. If you only want one loaf, the other will freeze successfully.

Begin this the evening before by placing all the fruits, including the candied peel, in a bowl, then dissolve the sugar in the hot tea, pour this over the fruits, cover the bowl and leave it overnight so the fruits become plump and juicy.

The next day, pre-heat the oven to gas mark 3, 325°F (170°C), then place the nuts on a baking sheet and pop them into the oven for 6-8 minutes (use a timer, as they burn easily). Then, when they're cool, roughly chop them.

Next, add the beaten egg mixture to the bowl containing the fruits. Then sift in the flour, add the toasted nuts and give everything a really good mixing. Now divide the mixture between the prepared loaf tins and bake them in the centre of the oven for 1¼-1½ hours, until they feel springy in the centre. Straightaway, loosen them with a palette knife and turn them out on to a wire rack to cool. Then have patience – it won't be long before you can taste some.

Quick Apricot, Apple and Pecan Loaf
Serves 8

6 oz (175 g) ready-to-eat dried apricots, each chopped in half

6 oz (175 g) Bramley cooking apple (1 medium apple), cut into ½ inch (1 cm) chunks, with skin on

6 oz (175 g) pecan nuts

a pinch of salt

1½ teaspoons baking powder

2 rounded teaspoons ground cinnamon

4 oz (110 g) wholemeal flour

4 oz (110 g) plain flour

4 oz (110 g) butter, at room temperature

6 oz (175 g) soft brown sugar

2 large eggs, beaten

3 tablespoons milk, plus a little extra, if needed

For the topping

4 cubes demerara sugar, roughly crushed

¼ teaspoon ground cinnamon

You will also need a 2 lb (900 g) loaf tin, lightly buttered.

Pre-heat the oven to gas mark 4, 350°F (180°C).

If you've never made a cake in your life before, I promise you that you can make this one – whether you're male, female, age six or 106, it really is dead simple, but tastes so divine you would think it took oodles of skill. The only important thing to remember (as with all cakes) is to use the right-sized tin.

First of all, when the oven has pre-heated, spread the nuts out on a baking sheet and toast them lightly for about 6-8 minutes, using a timer so that you don't forget them. After that, remove them to a chopping board, let them cool a bit, then chop them roughly.

Meanwhile, take a large mixing bowl, sift the salt, baking powder, cinnamon and both flours into it, holding the sieve up high to give the flour a good airing and adding the bran from the sieve to the bowl as well. Then simply add all the rest of the ingredients except the fruit and nuts. Take an electric hand whisk, begin to beat the mixture on a slow speed, then increase the speed to mix everything thoroughly till smooth, before lightly folding in the apricots, apple and pecans.

When it's all folded in, add a drop more milk, if necessary, to give a mixture that drops easily off the spoon when you give it a sharp tap, then pile the mixture into the tin, level the top and sprinkle on the crushed sugar cubes and cinnamon. Bake in the centre of the oven for 1¼-1½ hours or until the cake feels springy in the centre. After that, remove it from the oven, let it cool for about 5 minutes before turning it out on to a wire tray. Let it get completely cold before transferring it to a cake tin, which may not be needed if there are people around, as this cake tends to vanish very quickly!

Bara Brith
Serves 8

8 fl oz (225 ml) milk

2 oz (50 g) light brown soft sugar plus 1 teaspoonful

4 teaspoons dried yeast (not easy-blend)

1 lb (450 g) strong white bread flour, plus a little extra for rolling out

1 teaspoon salt

3 oz (75 g) butter

1 teaspoon ground mixed spice

1 large egg, beaten

12 oz (350 g) mixed dried fruit

clear honey, to glaze

You will also need a 2 lb (900 g) loaf tin, well buttered.

There are several different versions of this Welsh 'speckled bread'. Many of them don't contain yeast; but, for me, this version is the nicest and if there's any left over it's delicious toasted. In my Welsh childhood, I remember it made with yeast, very spicy and spread with lots of butter. Please note that easy-blend yeast is not suitable for this recipe.

First, warm the milk in a small saucepan till it's hand-hot, and then pour it into a bowl. Whisk in the teaspoon of sugar, followed by the yeast, then leave it in a warm place to froth for about 15 minutes.

Now sift the flour and salt into a large mixing bowl, stirring in the remaining 2 oz (50 g) sugar as well. Then rub the butter into the dry ingredients until the mixture looks like fine breadcrumbs. Stir in the mixed spice next, then pour in the beaten egg and frothed yeast, and mix to a dough. Now turn the dough on to a floured surface and knead until smooth and elastic (about 10 minutes), then replace the dough in the bowl and cover with a damp cloth or some clingfilm. Leave in a warm place to rise until it has doubled in size – about 1½ hours.

After that, turn the dough out and knock it down to get the air out, then gradually knead the fruit in and pat out to a rectangular shape to fit the width of the tin. Roll it up from one short side to the other and put it in the loaf tin (seam-side down). Place the tin inside an oiled plastic bag and leave it to rise, until the dough has rounded nicely above the edge of the tin (about 30-45 minutes).

Meanwhile, pre-heat the oven to gas mark 5, 375°F (190°C). When the dough has risen and springs back when pressed lightly with a floured finger, remove the bag; transfer the loaf to the oven and bake on the shelf below centre for 30 minutes. Then cover the top of the loaf tin with foil to prevent it over-browning, and continue to bake for a further 30 minutes. Turn the loaf out, holding it in a tea cloth in one hand and tapping the base with the other. It should sound hollow – if not, pop it back upside down (without the tin) for 5 minutes more. Cool the loaf on a wire rack, and brush the top with clear honey to make it nice and sticky, before the loaf cools. Slice thinly and serve buttered.

Banana and Walnut Loaf
Serves 8

4 medium bananas
(about 12 oz/350 g)

6 oz (175 g) walnut pieces

a pinch of salt

1 rounded teaspoon baking powder

1 teaspoon ground cinnamon

4 oz (110 g) plain flour

4 oz (110 g) wholemeal flour

grated zest of 1 orange
and 1 lemon

4 oz (110 g) butter,
at room temperature

6 oz (175 g) dark brown soft sugar

2 large eggs, at room temperature

a little milk, if needed

1 tablespoon demerara sugar
for topping

You will also need a 2 lb (900 g)
loaf tin, lightly buttered.

Pre-heat the oven to gas mark 4,
350°F (180°C).

This is a lovely, moist cake that keeps well and is perfect for picnics or packed lunches. In the summer it's brilliant served cut in thick slices and spread with clotted cream.

Begin by lightly toasting the nuts on a baking tray in the oven for 7-8 minutes (use a timer). Then let them cool before roughly chopping them. Now peel and mash 3 of the bananas to a purée, and peel and chop the other one into ½ inch (1 cm) chunks. Next, in a mixing bowl, sift the salt, baking powder, cinnamon and flours, holding the sieve up high to give everything a good airing (adding any bran left in the sieve).

Now add the remaining ingredients (except the chopped banana, nuts and demerara sugar) and, using an electric hand whisk, beat until everything is well mixed. Then lightly fold in the chopped banana and walnuts.

You may need to add a drop of milk to give a mixture that drops easily off a spoon when you give it a sharp tap. Now pile the mixture into the tin, level the top and sprinkle on the sugar. Then bake in the centre of the oven for 1¼-1½ hours, until the loaf feels springy in the centre. Let it cool for 5 minutes before serving.

Stollen

Stollen
Serves 10-12

5 fl oz (150 ml) milk

2 oz (50 g) golden caster sugar

2 teaspoons dried yeast
(not easy-blend)

12 oz (350 g) strong white
bread flour

¼ teaspoon salt

4 oz (110 g) very soft butter

1 large egg, beaten

1½ oz (40 g) currants

2 oz (50 g) sultanas

1½ oz (40 g) ready-to-eat
dried apricots, chopped

1 oz (25 g) glacé cherries, rinsed,
dried and quartered

1 oz (25 g) mixed whole candied
peel, finely diced

1 oz (25 g) almonds, chopped

grated zest of ½ lemon

6 oz (175 g) marzipan

For the glaze

4 oz (110 g) icing sugar, sifted

1 tablespoon lemon juice

You will also need a large baking
sheet, lightly greased.

At Christmas time in Austria they traditionally serve something called stollen: it is a rich, fruity yeast bread filled with marzipan and topped with a light glacé icing. If it is not all eaten when it's fresh you can also lightly toast it in slices.

Warm the milk, first of all, till you can just still dip your little finger in it. Then pour it into a glass jug, add 1 teaspoon of the sugar, along with the dried yeast, and leave it until it forms a frothy head of about 1 inch (2.5 cm). Meanwhile, sift 11 oz (315 g) of the flour, together with the salt and remaining sugar, into a large mixing bowl, and make a well in the centre. Pour the milk and yeast mixture into this, then add the butter and beaten egg. Mix everything together either with your hands or with a wooden spoon – until the mixture is well blended and leaves the side of the bowl cleanly. Then work in the fruits, peel, nuts and lemon zest, distributing them as evenly as possible. Knead the dough on a work surface for 5 minutes until it is springy and elastic. Now place the dough in a large, clean bowl and leave it in a warm place, covered with clingfilm (that has been lightly oiled on the side that is facing the dough) until it has doubled in size. The time this takes can vary, depending on the temperature – it could take up to 2 hours.

After that, turn the risen dough out on to a board floured with the reserved 1 oz (25 g) of flour, and knock the air out of it and knead the dough until it is smooth and elastic. At this stage, roll or press out the dough to an oblong 8 x 10 inches (20 x 25.5 cm). Using your hands, roll out the marzipan to form a sausage shape and place this along the centre of the length of the dough, finishing just short of the edges. Fold the dough over the marzipan and carefully place the whole thing on the baking sheet (with the seam underneath), allowing plenty of room for expansion. Leave it to prove, in an oiled polythene bag in a warm place, until it has doubled in size again. Meanwhile, pre-heat the oven to gas mark 5, 375°F (190°C). Bake the stollen for 35-40 minutes. Allow it to cool on the baking sheet for about 5 minutes before lifting it on to a wire rack to finish cooling. Next, make the glaze by mixing the sifted icing sugar with the lemon juice, then use a small palette knife to spread this all over the top surface of the stollen (while it is still warm). Serve as fresh as possible, cut into thick slices, with or without butter.

Sultana Loaf Cake
Serves 8

8 oz (225 g) sultanas

6 fl oz (175 ml) cold tea

8 oz (225 g) self-raising flour

a pinch of salt

6 oz (175 g) demerara sugar

1 large egg

You will also need a 2 lb (900 g) loaf tin, very well buttered.

Pre-heat the oven to gas mark 4, 350°F (180°C).

This is such a simple little recipe that a child could very easily make it and if, once made, you can possibly bear to wait, you'll find it improves with two days' keeping.

Begin by placing the sultanas in a large bowl and pouring the cold tea on them, then leave them to soak for about 5 hours, or, preferably, overnight. After soaking, the sultanas will have become large, plump and juicy.

Then simply sift the flour into the sultana mixture and stir it in, along with the salt and sugar. Beat the egg and stir this in too. Don't worry about the absence of fat in this recipe because with the high fruit content it does end up a very moist cake. Now spoon the mixture into the prepared tin, spread it out evenly and bake the cake on the middle shelf of the oven for about 1 hour. Then leave it in the tin for 10-15 minutes before turning out. Cool and store in an airtight tin till needed and serve in slices spread with butter.

Traditional Oatmeal Parkin

Makes 9 squares

8 oz (225 g) medium oatmeal (available at wholefood shops)

7 oz (200 g) molasses

4 oz (110 g) butter

4 oz (110 g) dark brown soft sugar

4 oz (110 g) self-raising flour

2 teaspoons ground ginger

a pinch of salt

1 large egg, beaten

1 tablespoon milk

You will also need a 7 inch (18 cm) square tin, 1½ inches (4 cm) deep, lightly greased, and lined with baking parchment.

Pre-heat the oven to gas mark 1, 275°F (140°C).

Real oatmeal parkin is unbeatable, but do make sure you leave it at least a week before eating – that way it will become much more moist and sticky than when it was first cooked. Originally, it was kept in proper wooden parkin boxes, but nowadays a tin will do instead.

First, weigh a saucepan on the scales, and weigh the molasses into it. Then add the butter and the sugar into the saucepan and place it over a gentle heat until the butter has melted down – don't go away and leave it unattended, because for this you don't want it to boil.

Meanwhile, measure the oatmeal, flour and ginger into a mixing bowl, add a pinch of salt, then gradually stir in the warmed syrup mixture till the mixture is all thoroughly blended. Next, add the beaten egg, and lastly, the milk.

Now pour the mixture into the prepared tin and bake on the centre shelf of the oven for 1¾ hours. Then cool the parkin in the tin for 30 minutes before turning out. Don't worry too much if the parkin sinks slightly in the middle – it sometimes happens in Yorkshire too, I'm told.

Marmalade Cake
Serves 8

1 rounded tablespoon chunky marmalade

8 oz (225 g) plain wholemeal flour, sifted

1 tablespoon baking powder

4 oz (110 g) dark brown soft sugar

4 oz (110 g) soft butter

grated zest of ½ large lemon

grated zest of ½ large orange

1 teaspoon ground mixed spice

4 oz (110 g) mixed dried fruit

5 fl oz (150 ml) milk, plus a little extra, if needed

1 teaspoon cider vinegar or white wine vinegar

1 tablespoon demerara sugar

You will also need a 1 lb (450 g) loaf tin, buttered, and the base lined with baking parchment.

Pre-heat the oven to gas mark 4, 350°F (180°C).

This delicious cake has a tendency to crumble, but if you wrap it in foil and store for a day or two you will find it cuts very nicely then.

In a large mixing bowl combine the flour, baking powder and dark brown soft sugar, then rub the butter into the dry ingredients until the mixture resembles coarse breadcrumbs. Next, add the grated lemon and orange zests, the mixed spice and dried fruit.

Stir everything together well, then add the milk, a little at a time, followed by the vinegar. Stir until all the ingredients are evenly distributed, and finally, stir in the marmalade. You should now have a good dropping consistency, so that when you tap a spoonful of the mixture on the side of the bowl, it drops off easily (you can adjust this with a touch more milk, if necessary).

Spread the mixture evenly in the prepared tin and sprinkle the top with the demerara sugar. Bake in the centre of the oven for 1¼ hours or until the cake has shrunk slightly from the sides of the tin and feels firm in the centre. Leave to cool in the tin for 10 minutes before turning out on to a wire cooling rack.

Sticky Malt Loaf
Makes 2 loaves (each serves 4-6)

4 tablespoons malt extract
(available from health food shops)

1 lb (450 g) plain flour

1 teaspoon salt

2 teaspoons easy-blend dried yeast

8 oz (225 g) sultanas

1 teaspoon dark brown soft sugar

2 tablespoons black treacle

1 oz (25 g) soft butter

2 teaspoons clear, runny honey
or golden syrup, to glaze

You will also need two
1 lb (450 g) loaf tins,
brushed with melted butter.

This, being a very rich yeast dough, takes a long time to rise but, provided you're not in a hurry, is very simple. When making two loaves, the easiest way to make sure you have the same amount of mixture in both tins is to place both the tins on balance scales – one where the weights should normally go and one on the scale pan – then you can balance the mixture perfectly. If you want to you can make one loaf in a 2 lb (900 g) loaf tin, just allow an extra 5 minutes' cooking time.

No pre-heating temperature because it's not needed till much later! First, sift the flour, salt and yeast into a bowl and stir in the sultanas. Then put the sugar into a glass measuring jug and pour in 8 fl oz (225 ml) hand-hot water and stir well. Now combine the malt extract, treacle and butter together in a small saucepan and heat gently until the fat melts. Then take the pan from the heat and leave it until the mixture is just warm.

Next, pour the warm water mixture and barely warm syrup mixture on to the flour and mix very thoroughly to a soft, sticky dough. Now spoon an equal quantity of the mix into the prepared tins. Level off the mixture, using the back of a spoon.

Place the tins in a large, oiled polythene bag. Trap a little air in the bag so it balloons up and the plastic is not in contact with the top of the tins. Then seal the bag and leave in a warm place to rise to the top of the tins. This will take between 3 and 4 hours, depending on the warmth.

Now bake the loaves at gas mark 5, 375°F (190°C) for 40 minutes. Turn the loaves out of the tins and tap the bases – they should sound hollow. If not, return them to the oven upside down without the tins for a further 5 minutes. Then brush the loaves with honey or golden syrup and leave them to cool on a wire rack before slicing and buttering.

Small Cakes Scones Cakes Muffins

Viennese Tartlets
Makes 16

8 oz (225 g) soft butter

3 oz (75 g) icing sugar, sifted, plus a little extra for dusting

7 oz (200 g) self-raising flour, sieved

2 oz (50 g) cornflour

about 3 tablespoons raspberry jam

You will also need a 12 hole and a 6 hole patty tin (with 16 of the holes lined with paper cake cases), and a large nylon piping bag, fitted with a large (½ inch/1 cm) rosette nozzle.

Pre-heat the oven to gas mark 4, 350°F (180°C).

These are very short little cakes with a nice crumbly texture.

First of all, beat the butter and icing sugar together until very soft and creamy and afterwards, stir in the sieved flour and cornflour to form a soft paste. Now sit the piping bag in an empty jug – nozzle end down – and fold the ends of the piping bag all round the edge of the jug. This leaves you with two hands free to transfer the paste to the piping bag. When it's all in, squeeze the paste down the bag to the nozzle and pipe the mixture into the paper cases in a circular pattern to give a hollow in the centre – you'll need to scrape the paste down the bag once or twice during piping, and to do this simply lay the bag down flat on the work surface and use a stiff plastic spatula or palette knife to push the mixture inside towards the nozzle end. Then carry on piping.

Bake the cakes for 20 minutes or until lightly golden brown, they will still be just slightly soft in the centre so don't worry about that. Remove them from the patty tins to a wire rack to cool for 15 minutes, leaving them in their paper cases.

Now put a small blob (about half a teaspoonful) of raspberry jam in the centre of each tartlet, then sift a light dusting of icing sugar over the top of each one and leave them to cool. It doesn't matter if the icing sugar obscures the jam – it will soon be absorbed by the jam so you'll end up with delicious little red blobs in the centre. Store the tartlets in an airtight tin.

Rich Fruit Scones
Makes 12

2 oz (50 g) mixed dried fruit

8 oz (225 g) self-raising flour

a pinch of salt

1½ oz (40 g) golden caster sugar

3 oz (75 g) butter,
at room temperature

1 large egg, beaten

3-4 tablespoons buttermilk, to mix

a little extra flour for rolling out
and for dusting tops

You will also need a lightly
greased baking sheet and
a 2 inch (5 cm) cutter.

Pre-heat the oven to gas mark 7,
425°F (220°C).

These tempting little scones are so quick and easy to make that you can have them on the table in less than half an hour after you'd first thought about making them. Don't worry if you can't get buttermilk, just use ordinary milk.

Begin by sifting the flour and salt into a bowl and sprinkling in the sugar, then rub the butter in lightly until the mixture looks crumbly. Now sprinkle in the dried fruit, pour in the beaten egg and add 3 tablespoons of the buttermilk. Start to mix the dough with a knife and finish off with your hands – it should be soft but not sticky, so add more milk, a teaspoon at a time, if the dough seems too dry.

Next, form the dough into a ball and turn it out on to a lightly floured work surface. Now roll it out very lightly to a round at least 1 inch (2.5 cm) thick, then cut the scones out by placing the cutter on the dough and giving it a sharp tap. Don't twist the cutter, just push the dough out, then carry on until you are left only with trimmings – roll these and cut an extra scone. Then place the scones on the lightly greased baking sheet and dust lightly with the extra flour.

Bake the scones in the top half of the oven for 10-12 minutes or until they are well risen and golden brown. After that, remove them to a cooling tray and serve very fresh, split and spread with butter.

Buttermilk Scones with West Country Clotted Cream and Raspberry Butter

Makes about 10

For the scones

2-3 tablespoons buttermilk,
plus a little extra for brushing

8 oz (225 g) self-raising flour,
plus a little extra for rolling out
and for dusting

a pinch of salt

3 oz (75 g) butter,
at room temperature

1½ oz (40 g) golden caster sugar

1 large egg, beaten

clotted cream, to serve

For the raspberry butter

1 lb (450 g) raspberries

6 oz (175 g) golden granulated
sugar

You will also need a lightly greased
baking sheet, and a 2 inch (5 cm)
pastry cutter.

Pre-heat the oven to gas mark 7,
425°F (220°C).

These are the lightest little scones you'll ever come across. But what is raspberry butter, you're wondering? The answer is that, traditionally, country people used to use up surplus summer fruits by making fruit cheeses. Damsons, for instance, can be cooked long and slow until they are concentrated into a thick, cheese-like consistency. Fruit butters are similar, but not quite so thick. This version, made with raspberries, has all the concentrated flavour and aroma of the fruit, perfect for piling on to scones with generous amounts of clotted cream. It can be kept in the fridge for a couple of weeks. The scones, however, don't keep well, so, in the unlikely event of there being any left, pop them in the freezer. They are also lovely eaten with cream and home-made jam.

To make the raspberry butter, purée the raspberries in a food processor, then pass them through a fine nylon sieve, pressing with a wooden spoon so that as much juice as possible gets through – you should get about 15 fl oz (425 ml). Now place the purée in a medium saucepan with the sugar and heat very gently until the sugar has dissolved. Then turn up the heat so the mixture boils rapidly for 8-10 minutes, but keep stirring from time to time so it doesn't catch on the base. When it's ready, the mixture should have reduced by one-third and a wooden spoon drawn across the base of the pan should leave a trail for 1-2 seconds only, but be careful not to overcook it, or you will get glue. Then pour it into a serving dish and leave to one side to cool and set for at least an hour.

For the scones, begin by sifting the flour and salt into a bowl, rub the butter lightly into the mixture until it looks like breadcrumbs, then add the sugar. Now, in a jug, beat the egg and 2 tablespoons of the buttermilk together and start to add this to the rest, mixing the dough with a palette knife. When it begins to come together, finish off with your hands — it should be soft but not sticky (if the dough seems too dry, add a little more buttermilk, a teaspoon at a time).

When you have formed the dough into a ball, tip it on to a lightly floured surface and roll it into a circle at least 1 inch (2.5 cm) thick – be very careful not to roll it any thinner; the secret of well-risen scones is to start off with a thickness of no less than an inch. Cut out the scones by placing the cutter on the dough and giving it a sharp tap – don't twist it, just lift it up and push the dough out. Carry on until you are left with the trimmings, then bring these back together to roll out again until you can cut out the last scone.

Place the scones on the baking sheet, brush them lightly with buttermilk and dust with a little flour. Now bake on the top shelf of the oven for 10-12 minutes, or until they are well risen and golden brown, then remove them to a wire rack to cool. Serve the scones thickly spread with raspberry butter and lots of clotted cream.

Hot Cross Buns
Makes 12

For the buns

1 lb (450 g) strong plain white
flour, plus a little extra, if needed

1 teaspoon salt

1 teaspoon ground mixed spice

½ teaspoon ground cinnamon

½ teaspoon freshly grated nutmeg

2 x 7 g sachets easy-blend yeast

2 oz (50 g) golden caster sugar

4 oz (110 g) currants

2 oz (50 g) mixed whole candied
peel, chopped

5 fl oz (150 ml) hand-hot milk

1 large egg, beaten

2 oz (50 g) butter, melted

For the crosses and the glaze

2 oz (50 g) plain flour

For the glaze

2 tablespoons granulated sugar

You will also need a baking sheet,
greased, and a large polythene
bag, the inside lightly oiled.

Hot cross buns cannot be dashed off quickly but kneading the dough and watching it rise is all very satisfying, and then your family can enjoy all that fruity, spicy stickiness!

First of all, sift the flour, salt, mixed spice, cinnamon and nutmeg into a large mixing bowl. Then sprinkle in the yeast and caster sugar, followed by the currants and mixed peel. Mix everything together evenly. Then make a well in the centre and pour in the milk and 1½-2 fl oz (40-55 ml) warm water, followed by the beaten egg and melted butter.

Now mix everything to a dough, starting off with a wooden spoon and then using your hands when the mixture becomes less sticky. Because it is never possible to be exact with the liquid, as flour can vary, if you need to add a spot more water, do so – or, if you find the mixture is getting too sticky, sprinkle in a bit more flour. Then transfer the dough to a clean surface and knead it until it feels smooth and elastic – this will take about 6 minutes. After that, place the dough back in the bowl and cover the bowl with clingfilm (that has been lightly oiled on the side that is facing the dough). Leave it in a warm place to rise – it will take about 1½ hours to double its original volume. Then, pressing the air out of it, re-shape the dough. Now divide it into 12 round portions and place them on the greased baking sheet, leaving plenty of room around each one. Use a sharp knife to make a cross on the top of each bun. Then leave them to rise again, covering them with an oiled polythene bag. This time they will take about 30 minutes.

While that's happening, pre-heat the oven to gas mark 7, 425°F (220°C) and make the crosses. Form a paste with the flour and 1½ tablespoons water, then roll this out and cut it into ¼ inch (5 mm) strips. When the second rising time is up, brush the strips with water to make them stick and place them on top of the buns, along the indentations you made earlier. Put the buns on a high shelf in the oven and bake them for about 15 minutes. While they are cooking, make the glaze by slowly melting together the sugar and 2 tablespoons water over a gentle heat until all the sugar grains have dissolved and you have a clear syrup. As soon as the buns come out of the oven, brush them immediately with the glaze while they are still warm.

Lemon Curd Butterfly Cakes
Makes 12

For the cakes

6 oz (175 g) self-raising flour, sifted

a pinch of salt

4 oz (110 g) butter, at room temperature

4 oz (110 g) golden caster sugar

2 large eggs, at room temperature

1 dessertspoon lemon juice

grated rind of 1 lemon

icing sugar for dusting

For the filling

about 4 oz (110 g) home-made (see below) or good-quality bought lemon curd

For the lemon curd

2 large eggs

grated zest and juice of 2 large juicy lemons

6 oz (175 g) golden caster sugar

4 oz (110 g) unsalted butter, at room temperature, cut into small lumps

1 teaspoon cornflour

You will also need a 12 hole patty tin, lined with paper cake cases.

Pre-heat the oven to gas mark 5, 375°F (190°C).

These little butterfly sponge cakes are baked in small paper baking cases and filled with lemon curd. I have given the recipe for home-made lemon curd here – there is more than you will need for the cakes but it will keep for several weeks in a cool place or in the fridge.

To make the cakes, place all the ingredients (except the icing sugar) together in a large mixing bowl and, using an electric hand whisk, whisk everything together until you have a smooth, well-combined mixture, which will take about 1 minute. Then, using a spoon, drop an equal quantity of the mixture into the paper cases, and sit the cases in the patty tin – giving it two or three light taps to settle the cake mixture.

Now bake on the shelf just above the centre of the oven for 20-25 minutes or until the cakes are well risen and golden. Then remove them to a wire rack and leave to cool. If you are making your own lemon curd, begin by lightly whisking the eggs in a small saucepan, then add the rest of the ingredients and place the saucepan over a medium heat. Now whisk continuously, using a balloon whisk, until the mixture thickens – about 7-8 minutes. Next, lower the heat to its minimum setting and let the curd gently simmer for a further minute, continuing to whisk. After that, remove it from the heat and leave to cool.

When both the cakes and the lemon curd are cool, take a sharp knife and, leaving a ½ inch (1 cm) border around the edge, and cutting at an angle, remove a cone shape from the top of each cake. Cut each cone in half (top to bottom) and set aside. Fill the cavity of each cake with lemon curd then sit the two cone-shaped pieces of cake on top like butterfly wings. Dust lightly with icing sugar.

Fresh Apricot and Pecan Muffins
Makes 20 mini or 6 man-sized muffins

4 oz (110 g) fresh apricots, finely chopped

1 oz (25 g) pecan nuts, finely chopped and lightly toasted

3 oz (75 g) plain flour

3 oz (75 g) wholemeal flour

½ tablespoon baking powder

¼ teaspoon salt

1 medium egg

1½ oz (40 g) golden caster sugar

4 fl oz (120 ml) milk

2 oz (50 g) butter, melted and cooled slightly

½ teaspoon pure vanilla extract

½ teaspoon ground cinnamon

For the topping

2 oz (50 g) pecan nuts, finely chopped

10 demerara sugar cubes, crushed

You will also need two 12 hole mini muffin tins (or 1 x 6 hole standard muffin tin). The muffins can be baked with or without greaseproof muffin cases.

Pre-heat the oven to gas mark 6, 400°F (200°C).

I love American home cooking, and one of the things I feel Americans are particularly good at is baking (both at home and commercially). The American muffin reigns supreme – not like the British bread version but more like superior fairy cakes and oh so much easier to make and more of a treat. Like many other things in America they used to come big, but now that calorie-counting is here to stay there are mini versions, which means you can make lots of different bite-sized flavours. Although I think minis are more fun, it has to be admitted that my husband's local cricket team prefers something more substantial, so I've given you a choice.

Start off by sifting the flours, baking powder and salt into a large bowl. Then, in a separate bowl, mix together the egg, sugar, milk, melted butter and vanilla extract. Now return the dry ingredients to the sieve and sift them straight on to the egg mixture (this double sifting is essential because there won't be much mixing going on). What you need to do now is take a large spoon and fold the dry ingredients into the wet ones – quickly, in about 15 seconds. Don't be alarmed by the rather unattractive, uneven appearance of the mixture: this, in fact, is what will ensure that the muffins stay light.

Now fold the apricots, pecan nuts and cinnamon into the muffin mixture, again, with a minimum of stirring: just a quick folding in. Spoon in just enough mixture to fill each muffin cup (if you're not using papers, grease the tins well) and top with the chopped pecans and crushed sugar before putting into the oven.

Bake on a high shelf for 20 minutes for minis or 30 minutes for the larger ones or until well risen and brown. Remove the muffins from the oven and cool in the tins for 5 minutes before transferring to a wire rack (if they are in the paper cases remove them from the tins straightaway).

Cheshire Cheese and Chive Scones

Cheshire Cheese and Chive Scones
Makes 6

3 oz (75 g) Cheshire cheese, grated

1 rounded tablespoon freshly snipped chives

6 oz (175 g) self-raising flour, plus a little extra for rolling out

½ teaspoon mustard powder

½ teaspoon salt

a good pinch of cayenne

1 oz (25 g) butter, at room temperature

1 large egg

about 2½-3 tablespoons buttermilk

For the tops

a little milk for brushing

1 oz (25 g) Cheshire cheese, grated

a good pinch of cayenne

You will also need a well-greased baking sheet, 10 x 12 inches (25.5 x 30 cm), and a 2½ inch (6 cm) fluted cutter.

Pre-heat the oven to gas mark 7, 425°F (220°C).

I'm convinced cheese scones were invented to use up the last remnants of some wonderful cheese – in this case, Cheshire. When you're down to the last bit, that is the time to make these meltingly light, squidgy cheese scones. Serve them for tea on Sunday, warm from the oven, spread with lots of butter.

Start by sifting the flour into a bowl, holding the sieve up quite high to give the flour an airing, then add the mustard, salt and one really good pinch of cayenne. Mix them in thoroughly, then rub the butter in, using your fingertips, until it's all crumbly.

Now mix in the 3 oz (75 g) of grated cheese, along with the freshly snipped chives. Next, beat the egg with 2½ tablespoons buttermilk and gradually add it to the dry ingredients, mixing first with a knife, then with your hands to make a soft dough – if it seems a little dry, add another ½ tablespoon of buttermilk, or enough to make a smooth dough that will leave the bowl clean. It's important not to overwork the dough or the scones will be heavy.

Now transfer the dough to a flat, lightly floured surface and roll it out as evenly as possible to around 1 inch (2.5 cm) thick – be very careful not to roll the dough out too thinly. The secret of well-risen scones is to start off with a thickness no less than an inch (2.5 cm). Then, using the fluted cutter, cut out 6 scones. You may need to re-roll the dough to cut out all 6.

Now place them on the well-greased baking sheet, brush the tops with milk, then sprinkle a little grated cheese on top of each scone, along with a faint sprinkling of cayenne. Bake them on a high shelf for about 15-20 minutes until the scones are risen and golden brown. Then cool a little on a wire rack, but serve warm.

Eccles Cakes
Makes 18-20

For the quick flaky pastry

6 oz (175 g) cold butter

8 oz (225 g) plain flour, plus a little extra for rolling out

a pinch of salt

For the filling

3 oz (75 g) butter

5 oz (150 g) light brown soft sugar

5 oz (150 g) currants

1 teaspoon ground cinnamon

½ teaspoon freshly grated nutmeg

grated rind of 1 large orange

2 oz (50 g) mixed whole candied peel, finely chopped

To glaze

a little milk

caster sugar for sprinkling

You will also need 2 large baking sheets, greased, and a plain 3½ inch (9 cm) cutter.

These spicy currant pastries are, predictably, a northern delicacy – which are never better than when home-made.

To make the pastry take the butter out of the fridge, weigh out the required amount, then wrap it in a piece of foil and return it to the freezing compartment of the fridge for 30-40 minutes. Meanwhile, sift the flour and salt into a mixing bowl.

When you take the butter out of the freezer, hold it in the foil, dip it into the flour, then grate it on a coarse grater placed in the bowl over the flour. Keep dipping the butter down into the flour to make it easier to grate. At the end you will be left with a lump of grated butter in the middle of the flour, so now take a palette knife and start to distribute it into the flour – don't use your hands – just keep trying to coat all the pieces of butter with flour until the mixture is crumbly. Now add enough water to form a dough that leaves the bowl clean, using your hands to bring it all gently together. Pop the dough into a polythene bag and chill it for 30 minutes – this time in the main body of the fridge. Pre-heat the oven to gas mark 7, 425°F (220°C).

Meanwhile, prepare the filling by first melting the butter in a small saucepan. Then take it off the heat and stir in all the filling ingredients quite thoroughly and leave it to cool. Next, turn the dough out on to a lightly floured surface. Roll it out to about ⅛ inch (3 mm) thick, then, using the cutter, cut the pastry into rounds (you will need to re-roll the pastry a few times to cut out all the rounds). Put a slightly heaped teaspoon of filling on to each round, then brush the edge of half the circle of pastry with water and bring the other side up to seal it. Then bring the corners up to the centre and pinch to seal well. Now turn your sealed pastry parcel over, so that the seam is underneath, then gently roll it flat to about ¼ inch (5 mm) thick and pat it into a round shape.

Place half of the parcels on each of the greased baking sheets and, using a small sharp knife, gash each one diagonally, across the top, three times. Now brush them with milk and sprinkle with caster sugar and bake on the middle shelf in two batches, each for about 15 minutes or until golden brown. Then transfer them to a wire rack to cool.

Feta, Olive and Sun-blush Tomato Scones
Makes 12

3 oz (75 g) feta, cubed small, plus 2 oz (50 g) extra, crumbled, for topping

10 black olives, pitted and roughly chopped

2 oz (50 g) sun-blush tomatoes in oil (or same quantity of mi-cuit tomatoes and a tablespoon of olive oil)

6 oz (175 g) self-raising flour, plus a little extra for rolling out

2 oz (50 g) wholemeal flour

¼ teaspoon baking powder

¼ teaspoon cayenne pepper

¼ teaspoon mustard powder

2 tablespoons extra virgin olive oil

1½ teaspoons chopped fresh thyme

1 large egg

2 tablespoons milk

You will also need a baking sheet, 10 x 14 inches (25.5 x 35.5 cm), lightly greased, and a 2 inch (5 cm) cutter (plain or fluted).

Pre-heat the oven to gas mark 7, 425°F (220°C).

These are lovely served as a snack or savoury at tea-time. They also go very well as a companion to many soups for lunch.

First of all, drain the sun-blush tomatoes, reserving 1 tablespoon of oil. If you are using mi-cuit tomatoes, there will be no need to drain them. Either way, chop the tomatoes into small pieces.

Now sift the flours and baking powder into a large, roomy bowl, tip in any bran left in the sieve, then add the cayenne and mustard powder and, using a knife, work in the 2 tablespoons of olive oil, plus the reserved tablespoon of oil from the sun-blush tomatoes (or the oil from the mi-cuit tomatoes, if using). When the mixture looks like lumpy breadcrumbs, stir in the chopped thyme, cubed feta, olives and the tomatoes.

Next, in a separate bowl, beat the egg with the 2 tablespoons of milk and add half this mixture to the other ingredients. Using your hands, bring the mixture together to form a dough, adding a little more of the egg and milk as it needs it – what you should end up with is a dough that is soft but not sticky.

Now on a floured board, roll the dough out to a depth of 1 inch (2.5 cm). Then stamp out the scones, using the cutter. Put the cut-out pieces on the baking sheet and brush them with the remaining milk mixture.

Finally, top each scone with the crumbled feta, and put the baking sheet on the highest shelf of the oven to bake for 12-15 minutes or until they've turned a golden colour. Then remove them to a wire rack until they are cool enough to eat.

Richmond Maids of Honour
Makes 18

9 oz (250 g) block ready-made fresh puff pastry

flour for rolling out

8 oz (225 g) curd cheese

1½ oz (40 g) golden caster sugar

grated zest of 1 lemon

1 oz (25 g) ground almonds

1½ oz (40 g) whole candied lemon peel, finely chopped

1 large egg, plus 1 large egg yolk

about 2 tablespoons home-made (see page 84) or good-quality bought lemon curd

icing sugar for dusting

You will also need a 3¼ inch (8 cm) plain cutter, and two 12 hole patty tins.

Pre-heat the oven to gas mark 6, 400°F (200°C).

Rumour has it that these delectable little curd-cheese tarts were named after the maids of honour who served at Richmond Palace in the 16th century. True or not, they taste wonderful, made with crisp puff pastry and a filling of squidgy cheese and lemon curd.

Begin by cutting the block of pastry in half so that you have two squares, and then, on a lightly floured surface, roll each piece into a square of about 11 inches (28 cm). Next, using the cutter, cut out nine circles from each piece. Be careful as you do this – just give the cutter a sharp tap and lift it, don't be tempted to twist it. Now line the tins with the pastry rounds; you should have 18 altogether.

Then, in a bowl, combine the curd cheese, sugar, lemon zest, ground almonds and chopped candied peel, then beat the egg and egg yolk together in a separate bowl and add this to the rest of the ingredients. Mix very thoroughly with a large fork until everything is very evenly blended. Next, spoon half a teaspoon of lemon curd into the base of each pastry case – don't be tempted to add more, as it will bubble over during the cooking – then spoon a dessertspoon of the curd-cheese mixture on top of this.

Then, when all the mixture has been added, bake the tarts in two batches on the centre shelf of the oven for about 20-25 minutes, by which time the mixture will have puffed right up and turned a lovely golden brown colour.

Now take them out of the oven and transfer them to a wire rack to cool. Don't worry if you see them start to sink a little, that's absolutely normal. If you like, you can give them a faint dusting of icing sugar before you serve them.

Savoury Mini Muffins with Two Flavourings
Makes 24

For the muffins

10 oz (275 g) plain flour

1 tablespoon baking powder

1 teaspoon salt

2 large eggs

8 fl oz (225 ml) milk

For the goats' cheese, red onion and rosemary flavouring

½ oz (10 g) butter

2 oz (50 g) red onion, finely chopped

2 oz (50 g) goats' cheese, cut into ¼ inch (5 mm) cubes

2 teaspoons chopped fresh rosemary, plus 12 small sprigs for garnishing

For the Gruyère, sage and onion flavouring

2 oz (50 g) Gruyère, grated

2 teaspoons chopped fresh sage, plus 12 small leaves for garnishing

2 oz (50 g) spring onions, finely sliced

2 teaspoons Parmesan, grated

You will also need two 12 hole mini muffin tins, and 24 greaseproof mini muffin cases.

For a fresh approach to party nibbles, I offer you these magic little savouries that can be served warm from the oven or, if made in advance, frozen, defrosted and re-heated. First, some simple muffin mathematics: the basic muffin recipe makes 24, and after that there are two flavourings – each for half that quantity – which should be prepared first.

To start with, you need to prepare the two muffin flavourings. To make the goats' cheese, red onion and rosemary muffins, begin by melting the butter in a small saucepan and softening the onion in it for about 5 minutes. Then allow it to cool. Next, prepare and set aside the ingredients for the Gruyère, sage and onion muffins. Now pre-heat the oven to gas mark 6, 400°F (200°C) while you make the basic muffin mixture.

First of all, sift the flour, baking powder and salt on to a large plate, then take a large mixing bowl and sift the mixture again, this time into the bowl, holding the sieve up high to give the flour a good airing. Now, in a jug, beat 1 egg, then whisk it together with the milk. Next, fold all this into the flour, using the minimum number of folding movements. (Ignore the unpromising look of the mixture at this stage and don't overmix.) Divide the mixture equally between two bowls in order to add the two different flavourings.

Now return to the first flavouring and gently mix the onion into the muffin mixture in one bowl, along with the goats' cheese and chopped rosemary, folding in, as before, with as few strokes as possible. Next, add all the prepared ingredients for the second flavouring (except for the Parmesan) to the muffin mixture in the other bowl and fold them in in the same gentle way.

After that, arrange the muffin cases in the tins and spoon the mixture into them. You can pile the mixture quite high. Beat the second egg and brush the surfaces with it, then top the goats' cheese muffins with a sprig of rosemary, and the Gruyère muffins with the Parmesan and a sage leaf.

Then bake them for about 20 minutes, or until well risen and golden. Remove the muffins from the tins to a rack and eat as warm as possible.

Chocolate, Prune and Armagnac Mini Muffins
Makes 24

2 oz (50 g) pitted ready-to-eat prunes, chopped small, and soaked overnight in 2 fl oz (55 ml) Armagnac

5 oz (150 g) plain flour

2 tablespoons cocoa powder

1 dessertspoon baking powder

¼ teaspoon salt

1 large egg, lightly beaten

1½ oz (40 g) golden caster sugar

4 fl oz (120 ml) milk

2 oz (50 g) butter, melted and cooled slightly

2 oz (50 g) plain chocolate drops

For the topping

3 oz (75 g) plain chocolate drops

a little extra cocoa powder for dusting

You will also need two 12 hole mini muffin tins, and 24 greaseproof mini muffin cases.

Pre-heat the oven to gas mark 6, 400°F (200°C).

Tiny little chocolate bites – soft, light, with melted chocolate swirled on the top and a light dusting of cocoa. These are lovely served with coffee at the end of a meal.

The night before you are going to make the muffins, soak the chopped prunes in the Armagnac. The next day, start off by sifting the flour, cocoa powder, baking powder and salt into a large bowl. Then, in a separate bowl, mix together the egg, sugar, milk and melted butter. Now return the dry ingredients to the sieve and sift them straight on to the egg mixture (this double sifting is essential because there won't be much mixing going on).

What you need to do now is take a large spoon and fold the dry ingredients into the wet ones – quickly, in about 15 seconds. Don't be tempted to beat or stir, and don't be alarmed by the rather unattractive, uneven appearance of the mixture: this, in fact, is what will ensure that the muffins stay light. Now fold the chocolate drops into the mixture, along with the prunes and Armagnac – again, with a minimum of stirring; just a quick folding in.

Put a muffin case into each hole in the tins and divide the mixture among them, about 1 heaped teaspoon in each, and bake on a high shelf in the pre-heated oven for 10 minutes, until well risen. Then remove the muffins from the oven and cool in the tins for 5 minutes before transferring them to a cooling tray.

While they're cooling, place the chocolate drops for the topping into a small bowl. Then place this into a saucepan of barely simmering water without allowing the bottom of the bowl to touch the water, and leave the chocolate to melt. Then, when the muffins are cool enough to handle, spoon a little melted chocolate on to each one, then place it back on the cooling tray. Before serving, give them a dusting of sifted cocoa powder.

Tiny Cheese, Onion and Olive Scones
Makes about 28

1½ oz (40 g) Parmesan, grated

1½ oz (40 g) mature Cheddar, grated

1 medium onion, finely chopped

6 black olives, pitted and chopped

1 tablespoon olive oil

6 oz (175 g) self-raising flour, plus a little extra for rolling out

½ teaspoon salt

½ teaspoon mustard powder

½ teaspoon cayenne pepper

1 oz (25 g) butter, at room temperature

1 large egg

about 2-3 tablespoons milk

freshly milled black pepper

You will also need a baking sheet, lightly greased, and a 1¼ inch (3 cm) plain cutter.

Pre-heat the oven to gas mark 6, 400°F (200°C).

These make perfect canapés and are so moreish that I don't think your guests could possibly survive on just one. They are simple to make and freeze superbly once cooked, provided you defrost and re-heat them in a hot oven for about 4 minutes before serving. If you're making them on the day of serving, split them once they're cooled and spread with a little herb cheese or a creamy blue cheese like Cambozola. Warm them in a hot oven just before serving.

Fry the onion in the oil over a highish heat for about 5-6 minutes or until it's a nice brown caramel colour and darkened at the edges. Keep it moving about so that it doesn't burn. Now transfer it to a plate to cool.

While that's happening, take a large mixing bowl, sift in the flour, salt, mustard powder and cayenne, and add a good grinding of black pepper (the scones need to have a piquant bite). Now rub in the butter, toss in the cooled onion, the olives and two-thirds of the grated cheeses, forking them in evenly. Beat the egg and pour this in, mixing first with a knife and finally, with your hands, adding only enough milk to make a soft dough – it mustn't be too sticky.

Turn the dough out on to a lightly floured surface, knead it gently till it's smooth, then roll it out to about ¾ inch (2 cm) thick, being careful not to roll it too thinly. Next, use a 1¼ inch (3 cm) plain cutter for cutting: place it lightly on the dough and give a sharp tap to stamp out the scones. Lightly knead together and re-roll any trimmings. Then, when all the scones are cut, brush them with milk, top them with the remaining grated cheeses and bake them near the top of the oven for 10-12 minutes. Remove them to a wire rack to cool.

Slices

Biscuits

Bars

Gingernuts
Makes 16

1 slightly rounded teaspoon
ground ginger

4 oz (110 g) self-raising flour

1 teaspoon bicarbonate of soda

1½ oz (40 g) granulated sugar

2 oz (50 g) butter,
at room temperature

2 tablespoons golden syrup

You will also need a large
(or 2 small) baking sheet(s),
lightly greased.

Pre-heat the oven to gas mark 5,
375°F (190°C).

These are, like most biscuits, extremely simple to make at home and you'll wonder why you ever bought them.

Begin by sifting the flour, ginger and bicarbonate of soda into a mixing bowl, add the sugar, then lightly rub in the butter until the mixture is crumbly. Next, add the syrup and, using a wooden spoon, mix everything together to form a stiff paste.

Now divide the mixture into 16 pieces about the same size as each other and roll each piece into a little ball. Place them on the baking sheet(s), leaving plenty of room between them because they spread out quite a bit while they're cooking.

Then simply flatten each ball slightly with the back of a spoon and bake just above the centre of the oven for 10-15 minutes, by which time they will have spread out and cracked rather attractively. Cool on the baking sheet(s) for 10 minutes, then transfer to a wire rack to finish cooling and store in an airtight tin.

Chocolate Fudge Brownies
Makes 15

2 oz (50 g) dark chocolate
(70-75 per cent cocoa solids),
broken into pieces

4 oz (110 g) butter

2 large eggs, beaten

8 oz (225 g) granulated sugar

2 oz (50 g) plain flour

1 teaspoon baking powder

¼ teaspoon salt

4 oz (110 g) nuts, chopped
(these can be walnuts, almonds,
hazelnuts, or, best of all, brazils)

For the topping

3 oz (75 g) granulated sugar

3 fl oz (75 ml) evaporated milk

4 oz (110 g) dark chocolate
(70-75 per cent cocoa solids),
broken into pieces

1½ oz (40 g) butter

2 drops of pure vanilla extract

You will also need a cake tin,
6 x 10 inches (15 x 25.5 cm),
1 inch (2.5 cm) deep, greased,
and lined with baking parchment.

Pre-heat the oven to gas mark 4,
350°F (180°C).

These moist, chewy, chocolate nut squares beloved by native Americans make compulsive eating, I find, so I try not to make them too often! For a really wicked treat, cover the cooked brownies with chocolate fudge topping before cutting them into squares.

First, melt the butter and the 2 oz (50 g) of broken-up chocolate together in a basin fitted over simmering water on a very low heat, making sure the bottom of the bowl doesn't touch the water. Then simply stir in all the remaining ingredients, spread the mixture in the lined tin and bake for 30 minutes, or until a knife inserted in the centre of the mixture comes out cleanly. Then leave the mixture in the tin to cool.

For the topping, combine the sugar and evaporated milk in a heavy-based saucepan. Place the pan over a low heat and allow the sugar to dissolve, stirring frequently. When all the granules of sugar have melted, bring the mixture to the boil and simmer very gently for 6 minutes – this time without stirring. Take the pan off the heat, stir in the chocolate and keep stirring until the chocolate has melted. Finally, stir in the butter and the vanilla extract.

Now transfer the mixture to a bowl, cool, then cover with clingfilm and chill for a couple of hours until it has thickened to a spreadable consistency. When the brownies are cold, cover them with the chocolate fudge topping and then cut into 15 squares.

A brownie warning: we sometimes get letters about failed brownies. The problem is that people expect cakes, but they are not the same consistency as cakes: they are (as described above) moist and chewy.

Banana and Chocolate Chip Slice
Makes 12

2 large, very ripe bananas, peeled and roughly chopped into ½ inch (1 cm) pieces

3 oz (75 g) dark chocolate chips or same quantity dark chocolate, chopped small

9 oz (250 g) self-raising flour

5 oz (150 g) cold butter, cut into small cubes

5 oz (150 g) golden caster sugar

cocoa powder for dusting, if you like

For the topping

9 oz (250 g) cream cheese

¾ oz (20 g) golden caster sugar

2 teaspoons pure vanilla extract

You will also need a cake tin, 6 x 10 inches (15 x 25.5), 1 inch (2.5 cm) deep, greased, and lined with baking parchment.

Pre-heat the oven to gas mark 4, 350°F (180°C).

This recipe is adapted from one given to me by Tony Carver, the chef who cooks for Norwich City Football Club players at their training ground in Colney. He says make sure that you use really ripe bananas.

First of all, sift the flour into a large, roomy mixing bowl. Then add the butter and rub it into the flour until the mixture resembles breadcrumbs (you can do this stage in a food processor, if you like). Next, stir in the sugar, chopped bananas and the chocolate (don't be alarmed, it will look like a crumble mix).

Now press the mixture evenly into the greased and lined tin and bake it on the middle shelf of the pre-heated oven for 35-40 minutes or until it is firm to touch in the centre and lightly golden.

Leave the slice in the tin until it is cold. While the slice is cooling, make the topping by mixing all the ingredients in a bowl until light and fluffy, then cover with clingfilm and chill until needed.

To finish, remove the slice from the tin to a wire rack, spread the chilled topping over, dust lightly with cocoa powder, if you like, and cut it into 12 pieces. Store in the fridge if the slice is not all eaten in one go.

Scottish Butter Shortbread

Makes 12 wedges

6 oz (175 g) butter,
at room temperature

3 oz (75 g) golden caster sugar,
plus extra for dredging

6 oz (175 g) plain flour, sifted,
plus a little extra for rolling out

3 oz (75 g) fine semolina

You will also need an 8 inch
(20 cm) diameter, fluted
flan tin, 1¼ inches (3 cm) deep,
with a loose base.

Pre-heat the oven to gas mark 2,
300°F (150°C).

This is the real thing – it can't be made in a factory. Using the fine semolina gives the shortbread a wonderful crunchy texture, and the flavour is extremely buttery.

First of all, beat the butter in a bowl with a wooden spoon to soften it, then beat in the sugar, followed by the sifted flour and semolina. Work the ingredients together with the spoon, pressing them to the side of the bowl, then finish off with your hands until you have a smooth mixture that doesn't leave any bits in the bowl.

Next, transfer the dough to a flat, lightly floured surface, and roll it out lightly to a round (giving it quarter turns as you roll) about the same diameter as the tin, then transfer the round to the tin. Now lightly press the mixture evenly into the tin right up to the fluted edges (to make sure it is even you can give it a final roll with a small glass tumbler). Finally, prick the shortbread all over with a fork – or it will rise up in the centre while it's baking. Bake for 50-60 minutes on the centre shelf – it should have turned pale gold and feel firm in the centre.

Then remove it from the oven and, using a palette knife, mark out the surface into 12 wedges. Leave it to cool in the tin, then, when it's cold, cut it into wedges. Dredge with the sugar and store in an airtight polythene box or tin.

Oatmeal Biscuits
Makes 24

2 oz (50 g) medium oatmeal

6 oz (175 g) plain wholemeal flour, plus a little extra for rolling out

½ oz (10 g) light brown soft sugar

1 teaspoon baking powder

½ teaspoon salt

¼ teaspoon hot curry powder

4 oz (110 g) butter, at room temperature

about 1 tablespoon milk

You will also need a large baking sheet, lightly greased, and a 2¾ inch (7 cm) plain cutter.

Pre-heat the oven to gas mark 4, 350°F (180°C).

I think it's really nice to be able to offer home-made biscuits with cheese and these are lovely with some Stilton or strong Cheddar and crisp celery.

Simply combine all the dry ingredients together in a bowl, then rub the fat evenly in. Add just enough milk to give you a slightly wetter dough than you would require normally (say, for shortcrust pastry) – since this dough is prone to breaking, a little extra moisture is deliberately used to help to hold it together.

Next, turn the dough out on to a floured work surface and roll out to about ⅛ inch (3 mm) thick. Use the 2¾ inch (7 cm) cutter to cut out the biscuit rounds – re-rolling the trimmings and adding a drop more milk if the dough happens to become a little dry.

Place the biscuits on the baking sheet and bake them for 15-20 minutes until firm and lightly browned. Leave them to cool on the baking sheet for 5 minutes before transferring them to a wire rack to cool. Store in an airtight tin.

Flapjacks
Makes 10

4 oz (110 g) light brown soft sugar

6 oz (175 g) butter

1 dessertspoon golden syrup

6 oz (175 g) porridge oats

a few drops of almond essence

You will also need a 7½ inch (19 cm) square baking tin, 1½ inches (4 cm) deep, lightly greased.

Pre-heat the oven to gas mark 2, 300°F (150°C).

Everybody loves flapjacks and I think making them with whole oats – sometimes called 'Jumbo' oats – adds an extra dimension.

To start, place the sugar, butter and golden syrup together in a medium saucepan and heat until the butter has melted. Then remove the saucepan from the heat and stir in the porridge oats and a few drops of almond essence.

Now, press the mixture out over the base of the prepared tin, and bake in the centre of the oven for 40 minutes. Allow to cool in the tin for 10 minutes before cutting into oblong bars. Leave until cold before removing the flapjacks from the tin, then store in an airtight container.

Spiced Apple and Sultana Fingers
Makes 18

For the pastry

8 oz (225 g) soft butter

2 oz (50 g) golden caster sugar

1 large egg

12 oz (350 g) plain flour, sifted, plus a little extra for rolling out

For the filling

¾ teaspoon ground mixed spice

14 oz (400 g) Bramley cooking apple (1 large apple), peeled, cored and finely chopped

4 oz (110 g) sultanas

1 tablespoon cornflour

2 tablespoons dark brown soft sugar

1 teaspoon lemon juice

a little icing sugar for dusting, if you like

You will also need a shallow baking tin, 9 x 13 inches (23 x 32.5 cm), ½ inch (1 cm) deep, lightly buttered.

Pre-heat the oven to gas mark 6, 400°F (200°C).

This is a good recipe to make when the windfall apples are demanding attention in the autumn.

First, cream the butter and sugar until light and fluffy. Then lightly beat the egg, and beat it, a little at a time, into the creamed butter, then gradually work in the flour. Now place half of this pastry in the tin and press it out all over the base of the tin with your hands, then put the other half of the pastry in a polythene bag in the fridge.

Next, take a medium saucepan and in it mix the cornflour, brown sugar and ground mixed spice, and gradually blend in 5 fl oz (150 ml) of water, followed by the sultanas, chopped apple and teaspoon of lemon juice.

Bring the mixture slowly to the boil, then simmer very gently for 3 minutes, remove the pan from the heat and allow the mixture to cool. When it's cool enough, spread it carefully and evenly over the pastry base.

Now roll out the remaining pastry on a lightly floured board to the size of the tin, roll the pastry over the rolling pin and transfer it to the tin to cover the apple filling, pressing lightly round the edges to seal. Now into the oven with it for 20-25 minutes, or until the pastry is lightly golden. Then dust with icing sugar, if you like, and leave to cool in the tin before cutting into fingers.

Plum and Cinnamon Oat Slices

Plum and Cinnamon Oat Slices
Makes 15

1 lb (450 g) fresh plums

1 rounded teaspoon ground cinnamon

10 oz (275 g) plain wholemeal flour

5 oz (150 g) porridge oats

1 teaspoon salt

8 oz (225 g) butter

4 oz (110 g) light brown soft sugar

You will also need a baking tin, 6 x 10 inches (15 x 25.5 cm), 1 inch (2.5 cm) deep, lightly greased.

Pre-heat the oven to gas mark 6, 400°F (200°C).

This is really an all-fruit recipe – it's exceptionally good with plums, but I love it with fresh or dried no-soak apricots, or apples, raspberries and blueberries; in fact, you can add whatever is in season. It's wonderful served warm as a dessert with cream – you'd make it in a round 9 inch (23 cm) springform tin, in which case it can be cut into 8-10 wedges and served warm from the oven. It can also be served cold with ice cream, instead of cake with tea. It's also a great recipe for children to make, as it's so easy.

Start by cutting all the plums in half, around and through their natural line, give a little twist to separate the halves and remove the stones, then cut them into thin slices. Now place them in a bowl and toss them around with the cinnamon.

Next, mix the flour and porridge oats, together with the salt, in a mixing bowl, then melt the butter and sugar in a small saucepan over a fairly gentle heat, stirring from time to time until the butter has melted. Now mix the melted butter and sugar with the oat mixture, starting with a wooden spoon but finishing off with your hands so you end up with a lump of dough.

Now halve the dough and press one half of the mixture into the baking tin, pressing it firmly all over the base with your hands like a wall-to-wall carpet. Next, scatter the plums evenly over the surface, then top with the remaining oat mixture, again, pressing down firmly.

Now place the tin on the centre shelf of the oven and bake for 25-30 minutes, or a bit longer if you like the top really crispy. Then remove the tin from the oven and allow to cool for about 10 minutes before marking into 15 squares – to do this make two cuts lengthways, then four cuts widthways, and don't worry if they're not all even. Unless you want to serve these warm, leave to cool completely in the tin.

Coffee and Hazelnut Macaroons
Makes about 30

2 tablespoons powdered instant coffee

4 oz (110 g) blanched hazelnuts

8 oz (225 g) golden caster sugar

2 heaped teaspoons ground rice

2 large egg whites

You will also need 2 baking sheets and some edible rice paper.

Pre-heat the oven to gas mark 2, 300°F (150°C).

You can also make these as very tiny biscuits and serve them in cases as petits fours. If you leave out the coffee, these crunchy little hazelnut biscuits are excellent for serving with ice creams or jellies. They also freeze well, so it's useful to have a little stock of them.

First, the nuts need to be ground to a coarse meal consistency: this can be done in a food processor, using the 'pulse' action – but do be careful because one pulse too many and they become very oily. Alternatively, you can use a small-handled nut grinder. Put the ground nuts in a mixing bowl, together with the sugar and ground rice, and mix them well together. Then stir in the unbeaten egg whites and the coffee powder and continue to mix to a stiffish paste.

Now line the two baking sheets with the rice paper and put teaspoonfuls of the biscuit mixture on them, leaving room in between them for expansion during the cooking. Bake in the oven for 30-35 minutes or until they are crisp on top.

Leave to cool completely before lifting the biscuits from the baking sheet. Cut the rice paper around each biscuit and store in an airtight container until needed.

Apricot and Nut Crunchies
Serves 24

4 oz (110 g) ready-to-eat dried apricots, snipped

4 oz (110 g) butter

3 oz (75 g) demerara sugar

1 dessertspoon golden syrup or runny honey

4 oz (110 g) self-raising flour

1 heaped teaspoon ground cinnamon

a pinch of salt

4 oz (110 g) porridge oats

For the topping

1 oz (25 g) ready-to-eat dried apricots, snipped

½ oz (10 g) pecan nuts, toasted and chopped

You will also need 2 solid baking sheets, lightly greased.

Pre-heat the oven to gas mark 3, 325°F (170°C).

You can almost imagine sneaking in to quickly grab one of these from under the cook's nose. But you don't have to tiptoe around to enjoy these fantastically moreish biscuits for this recipe is, quite literally, kids' stuff – one of the quickest, easiest, and simplest recipes of all, and perhaps the best news is that the basic recipe is supremely adaptable, so you can alter it to more or less any combination of nuts, fruits, and spices that you want.

The easiest way to deal with the ready-to-eat apricots is to snip them into small pieces with scissors, so do this first. Now put the butter and sugar into a small saucepan and add the syrup or honey. The best way to do this is to warm the dessertspoon under a hot running tap, take the amount of syrup you need on the spoon and literally push it off with a spatula into the pan. Next, place the saucepan on a gentle heat and allow the sugar, butter and syrup to dissolve.

Meanwhile, sift the flour, cinnamon and salt into a mixing bowl, then add the porridge oats and snipped apricots. Mix everything evenly and, when the butter, sugar and syrup have melted, pour this in to join the rest. Now, using a wooden spoon, stir and mix everything very thoroughly, then switch from the spoon to your hands to bring everything together to form a dough. If it seems a bit dry, add a few drops of cold water.

Now take lumps of the dough the size of a walnut and roll them into rounds, using the flat of your hand. Place them on a worktop and press gently to flatten them out into rounds 2½ inches (6 cm) in diameter, then scatter the snipped apricots and chopped pecans on top and press these gently in. Then, using a palette knife, transfer half the biscuits on to a greased baking sheet and bake on the middle shelf of the pre-heated oven for 15 minutes.

While they cook, prepare the second batch of biscuits and place these on your other baking sheet. When the biscuits are ready, leave them to cool on the baking sheet for 10 minutes and then transfer them to a wire tray to finish cooling. Store the biscuits in a sealed container – if you have any left!

Peanut Butter Biscuits
Makes 20

4 oz (110 g) crunchy peanut butter

3 oz (75 g) butter,
at room temperature

4 oz (110 g) light brown soft sugar

6 oz (175 g) plain flour

1 medium egg

¾ teaspoon bicarbonate of soda

a little demerara sugar

You will also need a large
(or 2 small) baking sheet(s),
lightly greased.

Pre-heat the oven to gas mark 4
350°F (180°C).

Even to those who loathe peanut butter as a rule, I can really recommend these biscuits.

First of all, place all the ingredients (except the demerara sugar) in a bowl and mix them together to form a stiffish dough. Now shape lumps of the mixture with your hands to form walnut-sized balls (no need to use flour or anything – the mixture is dry enough to leave the hands clean). Next, tip a small heap of demerara sugar on to a work surface and place a ball of mixture in the sugar. Flatten it slightly, flip it over and place it (sugared side up) on the lightly greased baking sheets.

The biscuits will end up about 2 to 2½ inches (5-6 cm) in diameter, so allow enough room for expansion. Bake them in the centre of the oven for 15 to 20 minutes, or until the biscuits feel firm when tested with the fingertips. Leave them to cool and harden slightly on the baking sheet(s) before transferring them to a wire rack with the aid of a palette knife. Store them in an airtight tin.

Gingerbread Men
Makes 15

1 teaspoon ground ginger

3 oz (75 g) light brown soft sugar, sieved

2 tablespoons golden syrup

1 tablespoon black treacle

1 teaspoon ground cinnamon

1 pinch of ground cloves

finely grated zest of ½ orange

3½ oz (95 g) butter

½ teaspoon bicarbonate of soda

about 8 oz (225 g) plain flour, plus a little extra for dusting

about 2 oz (50 g) currants, if you like

You will also need 2 large baking sheets, lightly greased, and a 5½ inch (14 cm) gingerbread man cutter (or template).

Pre-heat the oven to gas mark 4, 350°F (180°C).

This very well-behaved dough can put up with quite a bit of punishment and is, therefore, ideal for children to play around with. Gingerbread men cutters are widely available but, if not, you can easily make a template out of stiff card and cut around it. For a children's party, instead of arranging currants along the bodies, leave some plain and then afterwards, when cool, pipe on icing for faces and names on to each biscuit.

Begin by putting the sugar, syrup, treacle, 1 tablespoon of water, the spices and the zest together in a large saucepan. Then bring them to boiling point, stirring all the time. Now remove the pan from the heat and stir in the butter, cut into lumps, and the bicarbonate of soda. Next, stir in the flour gradually, until you have a smooth manageable dough – add a little more flour, if you think it needs it. Now leave the dough – covered – in a cool place to become firm, approximately 30 minutes.

Now roll the dough out on a lightly floured surface to ⅛ inch (3 mm) thick and cut out the gingerbread men. Currants can be pressed into the dough to simulate eyes, noses, mouths and buttons down their fronts. Arrange them on the lightly greased baking sheets and bake for 10-15 minutes or until the biscuits feel firm when lightly pressed with a fingertip. Leave the biscuits to cool on the baking sheets for a few minutes before transferring them to a wire rack.

Conversions for Australia and New Zealand

Measurements in this book refer to British standard imperial and metric measurements.

The standard UK teaspoon measure is 5 ml, the dessertspoon is 10 ml and the tablespoon measure is 15 ml. In Australia, the standard tablespoon is 20 ml.

UK large eggs weigh 63-73 g.

Converting standard cups to imperial and metric weights

Ingredients	Imperial/metric
almonds, ground	6½ oz/185 g
almonds, whole/chopped	5 oz/150 g
apricots, dried, whole	6 oz/175 g
butter	9 oz/250 g
carrots, grated*	5 oz/150 g
cherries, glacé, whole	7½ oz/210 g
coconut, desiccated	3½ oz/95 g
coconut, fresh, grated	2½ oz/60 g
cornflour	4½ oz/125 g
currants	5 oz/150 g
dates, pitted, chopped	6½ oz/185 g
dried fruit, mixed	4½ oz/125 g
flour, plain	4½ oz/125 g
flour, self-raising	4½ oz/125 g
flour, wholemeal	5 oz/150 g
hazelnuts, chopped	4½ oz/125 g
honey	12 oz/350 g
oatmeal	4½ oz/125 g
pecans, chopped	4½ oz/125 g
pecans, whole	4 oz/110 g
porridge oats	4 oz/110 g
prunes, whole, pitted	8 oz/225 g
raisins	4½ oz/125 g
semolina	4½ oz/125 g
sugar, brown, soft*	8 oz/225 g
sugar, demerara	8 oz/225 g
sugar, golden, caster	9 oz/250 g
sugar, golden, granulated	9 oz/250 g
sugar, icing	4½ oz/125 g
sultanas	4½ oz/125 g
treacle/molasses/syrup	12 oz/350 g
walnuts, halves	3½ oz/95 g
walnuts, pieces	4½ oz/125 g

* Firmly packed

Liquid cup conversions

Imperial	Metric	Cups
1 fl oz	25 ml	⅛ cup
2 fl oz	55 ml	¼ cup
2¾ fl oz	70 ml	⅓ cup
4 fl oz	120 ml	½ cup
6 fl oz	175 ml	¾ cup
8 fl oz	225 ml	1 cup
10 fl oz	275 ml	1¼ cups
12 fl oz	340 ml	1½ cups
16 fl oz	450 ml	2 cups
1 pint	570 ml	2½ cups
24 fl oz	680 ml	3 cups
32 fl oz	1 litre	4 cups

A few ingredient names

bicarbonate of soda
baking soda

Bramley cooking apples
use green cooking apples

buttermilk
if unavailable, use ordinary milk

Cheshire cheese
crumbly-textured hard cheese

chocolate drops
chocolate melts

clotted cream
if unavailable, use thick cream

desiccated coconut
flaked, dry coconut

fromage frais
fromage blanc

ground almonds
almond meal

porridge oats
rolled oats

sugar, golden, caster/ granulated/icing
if unavailable, use caster/granulated/ icing sugar

Index

Caroline Arber 104
Patrice de Villiers 74, 82
Miki Duisterhof 6, 13, 19, 20, 31, 35, 42, 45, 48, 55, 60, 74, 99, 112, 122
Norman Hollands 9
Peter Knab 6, 26/7, 32, 41, 46, 74, 86, 91, 96,104, 125, 126, 130
James Murphy 64
Emma Neish 13
Miles New 17
Debbie Patterson 28, 56
Michael Paul 32
Simon Smith 81
Clive Streeter 6, 32, 74
Petrina Tinslay 5, 6, 10, 13, 14, 23, 24, 36/7, 38, 48, 51, 52, 56, 59, 62/3, 67, 68, 71, 72, 74, 77, 85, 88/9, 92, 95, 100, 103, 104, 107, 108, 111, 115, 116, 119, 120/1, 129, 133
Cameron Watt 78

Styling credits

Ici et Là (www.icietla.com.au)
TLC Treasures
(email: tlc_treasures4u@yahoo.com.au)
Très Fabu (00 61 2 9967 0099)
Major + Tom (00 61 2 9557 8380)
Mud Australia (www.mudaustralia.com)

Delia Smith is Britain's best-selling cookery author, whose books have sold over 18 million copies. Delia's other books include *How To Cook Books One, Two* and *Three, The Delia Collection*: *Soup, Chicken, Fish, Italian, Pork* and *Chocolate*, her *Vegetarian Collection*, the *Complete Illustrated Cookery Course, One Is Fun*, the *Summer* and *Winter Collections* and *Christmas*. She has launched her own website. She is also a director of Norwich City Football Club, where she is in charge of Canary Catering, several restaurants and a regular series of food and wine workshops.

She is married to the writer and editor Michael Wynn Jones and they live in Suffolk.

For more information on Delia's restaurant,
food and wine workshops and events, contact:
Delia's Canary Catering, Norwich City Football Club plc, Carrow Road,
Norwich NR1 1JE; www.deliascanarycatering.co.uk
For Delia's Canary Catering (conferencing and events enquiries),
telephone 01603 218704
For Delia's Restaurant and Bar (reservations),
telephone 01603 218705

Visit Delia's website at www.deliaonline.com